The Heartgasm Revolution

The Heartgasm Revolution

A MIND BLOWING GUIDE TO SELF LOVE

KIRSTEN JOHNSON

ISBN: 978-1-7330057-0-8 (Paperback)
ISBN: 978-1-7330057-1-5 (Audio)
ISBN: 978-1-7330057-2-2 (Kindle)

By reading this book, you understand that Kirsten Johnson is a certified professional life coach and the owner of Kirsten Johnson International. Our purpose is to inspire people to empower themselves into living their best life.

This book is for educational and entertainment purposes only. The information and education provided is not intended or implied to supplement or replace professional medical treatment, psychological or professional advice of any kind, and/or diagnosis.

Although we do our best to make sure all of the information contained herein is up to date and/or accurate, we do not make any representation that all the information contained herein is accurate or free of errors at all times. We do not assume any responsibility for accuracy of the book information, or its safety and efficacy as it applies to you. You should review any and all changes to your diet, lifestyle, exercise regimen, and mental health care with your physician or a medical professional before trying it yourself.

We do not offer any representations, guarantees, or warranties of any kind regarding the book in any way including but not limited to effectiveness, safety, harm, or results achieved as a result of your use of the book. The book is offered "AS IS" and without representations, guarantees, or warranties of any kind, including but not limited to, implied warranties of merchantability and fitness for a particular purpose, neither express nor implied, to the extent permitted by law. We are not liable for damages of any kind related to your use of the book or any information contained or discussed therein.

By using this book, you implicitly signify your agreement to all of the terms contained herein.

Cover design by Marisa Ravel of Laser Kitten and Giovanni Rossi
Front cover outfit by Gretchen Johnson, UNSUPERVISED Los Angeles
Front cover image by Brian Crawford
Back cover image by Gede Widarmana
Edited by Rebecca Dettorre

First printing edition 2019

https://kirjohnson.com/

DEDICATION

To Bill Wilson and Eckhart Tolle—

The two authors of the two books that transformed
my life the most.

Your words, your wisdom, your books gave me the tools to climb out of
a living hell, a time filled with addiction and
all-encompassing anxiety, a time when I'd frequently wake up
thinking, "Fuck—I'm still alive."

Your teachings guided me back to LIFE.

And I am eternally grateful.

GIVING BACK

There's something about Bali—an almost palpable loving energy—that's had me feeling *at home* here since first arriving in 2014. I've lived, loved and radically transformed my heart on this magical land. The idea for this book came while I was on Bali. And I learned to love myself here.

So I wanted to give back to the island that has given me so much. A search online for "Bali charity" brought me to a video from the John Fawcett Foundation. I watched as blind children saw their mothers for the first time post-surgery and elder folks who had gone blind see their grandchildren for the first time. Witnessing such miraculous beauty pierced my heart deeply, leaving me erupting with tears and overflowing with love—an experience I've come to call a heartgasm.

And now for YOUR heartgasm! I've aligned with the John Fawcett Foundation and your purchase of this book has helped to bring vision to an entire village on Bali. The mobile eye clinic performed sight restoring vision on 10 blind people, provided 223 glasses including to children at the village elementary school, and provided eye medication to treat 80 people with eye infections.

Thank you, dear reader.

You can watch our video here: kirjohnson.com/heartgasm

TABLE OF CONTENTS

HEARTGASMS? 3

INTRODUCTION 15

PART ONE:
YOUR BARRIERS TO LOVE 21

WHAT'S KEEPING YOU STUCK AF 27

FIGHTING FEELINGS 29

NUMB 30

HOLLYWOOD 31

THE BLAME GAME 33

EXCITEMENT JUNKIE 38

ADDICTIONS 39

RELATIONSHIPS 42

CURTAIN CALL 45

PART TWO: EXCAVATING YOUR HEART
YOUR MIND 49

Getting Your Mind Right 54

Evict the Victim 58

Shoulding All Over Yourself 63

Waiting for the Future 64

Taming the Caveman 65

SELF LOVE 71

    Be Your Own BAE 74

    All the Feels...75

    Mental Tsunamis 79

    You Are Not Your Feelings 83

    Cancelling the Guilt Trip..........................86

    Getting Your Shame Off 90

    Own Your Humanity................................98

    STOP Rejecting Yourself 100

    Total Acceptance 101

    Yesing Yourself 102

    Make Love to Yourself...........................106

    Bathroom Quickie 108

    Making Love 110

    Keeping the Vibe Alive...........................112

    Give Trees a Chance 116

YOUR BODY 117

    Roll It Out 117

    Shake & Chill 119

    Smiling on the Inside 120

LOVING OTHERS 121

    Bombing the Barriers..............................121

    Loving the Kindness 124

Provoking Compassion............................ 128

Love Generation................................... 131

Little Parents 138

PART THREE: COME ALIVE........................ 139

TRUST.. 141

Doubt Shit Storms................................. 141

Be Your Own Cheerleader 144

Believe in Yourself................................ 146

God's Billboard.................................... 149

Godgasms 150

ELIMINATE.. 152

Minimalism 152

Junk-Free Diet 156

Friend Detox 158

Divorce Your Story 161

CREATE 162

Have an Affair with Your Future Life.......... 162

Sexual Ideal....................................... 164

Hero 166

You-logy 167

YOLO 168

Feeling Foreplay 169

Vision Board 170

Creative Visualization...........................171

The Good Feels.....................................172

Pillow Talk 173

THE REVOLUTION 174

P.S. THE DOUBLE CHECK 175

AFTERWORD 180

ACKNOWLEDGEMENTS...............................183

    Books that Inspired
    the Healing of My Heart and
    Some of the Practices in this Book......................187

COMING SOON—*Elephant: A Memoir* 189

ABOUT THE AUTHOR.............................190

♡

heart·gasm

noun

An energetic explosion of the heart—where love, passion and aliveness flood the body along with strong feelings of warmth, connectedness and bliss, usually accompanied by tears of joy and a smile.

HEARTGASMS?

You want love and happiness. And now that you know what heartgasms are, you want them too.

You want to be multi-heartgasmic.

But it eludes us. We think we are moving towards love, with our striving, achieving, and proving our worth. But this is exactly what keeps us from getting it.

There's a better way.

This book is intended to inspire an opening in your mind. Actually, it's your heart that I'm aiming for. But our minds can often be the gateway to our hearts since most of us have mentally put our hearts on lockdown.

My biggest desire for this book is that it guides you in removing what's been blocking you from love.

You know, the kinda book you'd give your friend who is experiencing a breakup. Or a breakdown. A book you'd see at the airport, read on the flight, then feel a bit more connected to yourself. Or profoundly more connected to the truth of who—and what—you really are. A book you'd give your friend on her or his sobriety anniversary. A potential healing map. A sassy tool for your soul's evolution. Guidance during your dark night of the soul. Your way out of secondary addictions. All while you return to your natural, loving state.

This book is a practical guide for healing your heart, including *how* to love yourself more, so that you can experience more love, happiness, and aliveness.

Let's get the energy in your heart stirring now with some fun surprise bonuses! Ooo, you ready for it? I've created guided audios so you can get a deeper experience of the heartgasmic practices in this book.

Get your *The Heartgasm Revolution* companion audios and bonus content here: kirjohnson.com/heartgasm/

Like most of us, I wasn't always multi-heartgasmic. Back in the day, I was well on my way to what I thought was my American dream. I had completed a master's in statistics and was earning multiple six figures working for tech start-ups in San Francisco.

I was busy trying to look perfect on the outside.

Alcohol fueled this masquerade.

The buzz of booze silenced my anxiety and feelings of inadequacy, giving me a sort of liquid courage to pursue my dreams. Which of course was not sustainable. And even worse, it stopped working.

But I couldn't stop drinking.

Then there were the anxiety meds.

After a panic attack on the freeway, I went to a psychiatrist. He diagnosed me with just about every anxiety disorder: generalized anxiety disorder, panic disorder, post-traumatic stress disorder (PTSD), and freeway phobia. I was also terrified of public speaking and was afraid to leave the house.

He prescribed me the benzodiazepine klonopin. I took the benzos twice daily as advised and truly didn't think I was abusing them. But I'd lied to the doctor about how much I drank. And so my mental health continued deteriorating. And worse, I almost immediately became addicted to the benzos.

I had to keep taking them otherwise I'd be pummeled by a massive anxiety attack. The pills numbed the anxiety but they also numbed any feelings of joy or aliveness, leaving me trapped in a dark, living hell of fear, addiction, and declining mental health.

Then one depressing September day, I was walking through my apartment and caught my reflection in the hallway mirror.

> I looked into my eyes but it was like
> I was looking into an empty shell,
> as if the flame of my spirit
> was about to flicker out.

I was terrified.

Because I knew I was dying.

One week later, on September 29, 2009, I went to rehab.

In early sobriety, I learned how to cope with the anxiety attacks without benzos or booze. Then, a Guru in India taught me how to rewire my brain to rid myself of the anxiety disorders. I did the 12 steps several times and trucked along sober, living life on life's terms.

When I was about five years sober, and after much transformation, more was revealed—the stuff *under the hood*.

The shame.

It's like the buried shame had a wisdom to it. It stayed hidden until I learned how to transform the anxiety.

I'd later see that the anxiety was there because of the shame.

Shame used anxiety as a signal, like a warning light on the car's dashboard saying check under the hood, something deep down in the heart isn't right.

The anxiety indicated I was living inauthentically, which of course was because I was filled with shame.

A lot of my shame came from the trauma I endured from early sexual abuse. I wouldn't know it for decades, but I had PTSD from the abuse. And the "anxiety," the drinking, the not knowing who I was, and my major defense mechanisms like perfectionism, denial, and avoidance were related to that unhealed sexual trauma. I use quotes for "anxiety" because with wiser eyes, I can see that what I was actually experiencing was traumatic stress.

I never talked about the underlying sexual trauma. So my symptoms were diagnosed.

> To be branded with
> the stigma of mental illness
> while my symptoms of trauma
> were medicated
> kept me stuck.

Back then, I didn't have the courage to speak about my sexual trauma or the clarity to connect the dots between the trauma and my rapidly declining mental health.

The long-term effects of unhealed childhood sexual abuse and subsequent revictimization are a topic for another time…although heartgasms are a great healing tool on that path as well.

But if you're curious now, check out my TEDx talk called "The Secret That Almost Killed Me" on exactly that topic here: kirjohnson.com/tedtalk.

Back to my heart and shame.

What I found under my hood—unbeknownst to me until it smacked me across the face at five years sober—was the deeply hidden belief that *I'm unlovable.* I had only *thought* I loved myself. But upon reflection, it was vanity. I was loving the image I had created of myself.

I wasn't actually *being* loving with myself.

"The hood" popped open after a year-long spiritual journey throughout Southeast Asia. I moved to Bali, Indonesia in 2014 because of a wild experience I had with Bali's palm trees. While on vacation there, I spent afternoons sipping coffee and looking out from my hotel balcony at the palms.

The energy in my heart would stir then explode into a profound feeling of rapture. A few seconds later, I'd be left feeling deep grief. Tears would flow.

These—as I would later name them—heartgasms, were so intense and mysterious that they quite literally inspired me to go back home, sell and give away my stuff, and immediately move to Bali.

I know this sounds wild, but I had to find out what was happening with my heart.

Plus at that time I had just had surgery and was unable to work, so an extended stay on a healing island made a little logical sense.

I spent the first six months in Bali doing energy healing work. This was followed by an insane number of meditation courses while traveling for six months including vipassana in Thailand, a three-week meditation course at a Tibetan Buddhist monastery in Nepal, then a two-month stay at a meditation center in India.

I compulsively went deep until my denial was ripped off and I was plunged into a breakdown.

I can now see that a spiritual journey is a breakdown...a breaking down of everything that is NOT us.

In that sense, I not only asked for a breakdown, but it meant that the spiritual journey was a success.

By the time I got back to Bali, I was cracked wide open. With my denial stripped away, I was left with me. Unhealed me.

Broken-hearted me.

I spent the next four months crying in my little apartment surrounded by rice fields in Ubud, Bali. Nothing made sense anymore. Everything I believed no longer seemed true. I had been thrust into a long, dark night of the soul. My childhood wounding emerged and it came with an eruption of old, unhealed emotions.

It was the most beautiful time of my life.

Because it was the first time EVER that I actually loved myself. Many old stories and old emotions surfaced. I radically loved myself through it by allowing everything.

I made a firm commitment to no longer reject myself.

The sad thing is, until that point, I had no idea that I was constantly abandoning and rejecting myself.

I meditated daily with the palm trees (yea, I know, I know…) and the entire process became clear to me—the spiritual journey, the healing of the heart, the misdirected attempts most of us are doing to try to *get love* and *prove our lovability.*

This is everyone's journey, everyone who wants real love and real happiness.

> ## This is the journey of the human heart.

The wisdom I'm sharing with you in this book is what I learned about love, happiness, and aliveness in Southeast Asia.

Some of it is inspired by teachers and authors who I mention in the back of the book. All of it is inspired by what helped me transform my heart.

And of course, I am still very much a student on this path as well—the journey from living in the head to living from the heart.

And while sometimes I feel like I'm just getting started, or find myself lacking love for myself or others, the truth is that I've come a long way.

So instead of waiting until
I'm 100% loving, or some type of
"self-love expert," I'm sharing with you
what's helped me transform my heart,
and therefore my entire world,
thus far.

Because hey, it's obviously not practical for everyone to head to a tropical jungle and cry for four months. Or to take a spiritual journey across Asia for a year. Or to drop everything and move to Bali because a tree inspired her heart.

And who really wants to heal her heart anyway, or dive into her original pain?

Unless of course your heartbreak smacks you in the face and you're left without the ability to stop it or run... If that's you, welcome, you're not alone.

Or perhaps you're here to continue your heart-healing journey because you demand more for your life—more LOVE more PASSION more ALIVENESS.

Maybe you're not willing to wait for your pain to erupt, maybe just maybe you're a spiritual warrior, armed with a fierce determination to heal and enjoy your life to the fullest.

Either way, the path to living a juicy, heartgasmic life—a life filled with love, passion, and aliveness—is to heal what's blocking us from it.

I'm so glad you're here.

INTRODUCTION

We are all multi-heartgasmic.

> If you're not feeling the
> love, happiness, and aliveness
> you desire, it's likely that
> you're blocked.

But no worries, this book is about unblocking you. This book is a practical guide to feeling love.

I'm guessing your heart is ready to become multi-heartgasmic—that the Universe has brought you this book so that you can get free. And that your heart is ready to break down its protective barriers so that it can juice with joy, erupt with love, and explode with passion. Awesome.

Most of us spend our lives flatlined in boredom and discontent. We're afraid to be ourselves.

> We've been numbed out for years
> (or decades!) on alcohol, food,
> sex, shopping, the internet, working…

We're disconnected from ourselves. Lost. Not knowing who we really are. And with no clue how to reconnect back to ourselves.

It's like we've constructed armor, thick steel barriers, over our hearts. We wanted to keep our hearts safe.

But it doesn't work.

Imagine building a cement wall around a beautiful and fragile orchid. You want to protect it. But in reality, you're suffocating it by denying it vital nutrients. It's slowly dying but you can't tell because it's hidden far behind the wall.

Our hearts are more resilient than orchids. They can survive a long time after we close them off and seal them away behind armored barriers.

Some hearts spend their entire existence this way.

Eff that. Demand more for yourself, baby.

Free your heart. Let it explode with joy. Let it thrive in the sun and connect with others.

Let it love and be loved.

The intention of this book is to show you how.

Part One is about removing your barriers to love.

Part Two is about healing your heart back to its natural, loving state.

Part Three is about coming alive and thriving.

This process is like watering your beautiful heart, putting it in the sun, and letting it fully bloom.

This book is about LIVING fully.

All of my coaching clients—whether they come to me because they want to overcome anxiety, rocket their recovery, or launch their dream business—reveal their real desires within a few sessions:

They want love.
They want to be happy.
They want to feel joy.

They want to be FREE.

So let's cut to the heart of it—because
I'm guessing love, happiness, and
a joy-filled life are what you
actually want, too.

We start with ourselves.

Just like if we wanted to be more
orgasmic, we'd start by playing
with ourselves, *right?*

We'd explore what feels good, discover what turns us on,
what we like and what we don't like—or maybe that's
just what I did…

Once we become multi-orgasmic by ourselves, it's easier
to be multi-orgasmic with someone else.

Same goes for our hearts. We uncover, explore, and play
with our own hearts first, relax into our own love, then
we can share our love with others. Because I bet if you're
super honest with yourself, what you really want—
despite whatever your surface goal is—is to FEEL your
heart.

Let's get you there.

Err, here. Here is where we're going to get you. Because here is where love is. Here is where happiness is.

Thinking love and happiness could be in the future is part of what keeps us stuck, miserable, and unfulfilled.

This is how most of our human minds work though.

The trick then is to
COME ALIVE now.
To live now.

Bring us along for the ride!

Use #Heartgasm on Instagram so we can follow your heartgasmic journey. And you can find your fellow heartgasmic revolutionaries with that hashtag too.

It's time to come alive.
It's time to live.

PART ONE:

YOUR BARRIERS TO LOVE

*"Your task is not to seek for love, but merely to seek
and find all the barriers within yourself
that you have built against it."*
~ *Rumi*

Something brought you here.

A breakup, a dark night of the soul, anxiety, getting
sober, an unsatisfying career…

Or perhaps you're sober and caught in secondary
addictions like shopping, porn, people pleasing, food…

Or maybe you've been struggling in relationships,
struggling to feel happy, struggling with emotional
sobriety or feeling stuck.

If you've been feeling flat, it's likely you're in a rut, in a metaphorical ditch.

It's dark, cold, and loveless in this ditch of yours.

You may have been in there for such a long time that
you've forgotten that you're in a hole, forgotten what

living in the sunshine feels like. And no matter how much you pray, visualize, or affirm that the sun is shining, it's not gonna happen as long as you remain in the ditch.

Resigning ourselves to unacceptable circumstances put us in a ditch. We've got to climb out.

This means stop decorating the ditch. Stop talking about the ditch. Start to move out of it.

This book is your ladder. Unless—of course—you want to stay in the ditch.

Great, you're still reading. Let's get you out! Awareness that you're in a hole, that you've got circumstances or a situation you want to climb out of, is how you start to get out.

But how did you get in the ditch?

When you were young, there were times you felt rejected, ignored, uncared for, and abandoned.

This happened many times. From here, it was logical to decide that you must be lacking the attention, affection, connection, and love you craved because—something's wrong with you. Why else would mom and dad ignore and neglect you? You must not be good enough. The only conclusion your sweet, young mind could think of is that you must be unlovable.

This is crazy.

UNLOVABLE??!!
How could that possibly be true?
You are so lovable!

But we believe it.

It's obviously wrong. But as a kid, not getting the love we need, we conclude that we must not be worthy of love in the first place. Our parents cannot be wrong in our young eyes. Our lives completely depend upon these adults, after all.

This is how our hearts break.
From believing the worst lie of all.
From believing that
we are unlovable.

It's soul shattering.

And too painful to keep in mind...so we bury the lie down deep, beyond our conscious mind.

From here, since obviously we all need love, we each conclude these ass-backwards ideas:

1. I need to get love.

2. I need to earn love.

3. I need to prove I'm lovable.

The TRUTH, obviously, is:

1. You are LOVABLE.

2. Love is a feeling that comes from inside.

3. Only when we love ourselves can we love others.

4. When we give love, we receive love.

5. There's nothing—NOTHING—wrong with you.

> But, because we
> deep down believe the lie
> that we are unlovable, we start to
> experiment with how we can
> get the love we crave.

WHAT'S KEEPING YOU STUCK AF

We think to ourselves, *Hey look at this ditch, it's not so bad, I'll decorate it and add a little sparkle to it.*

Yep, we set up shop in the ditch. We resign ourselves to living in an unacceptable dark funk. We don't know any better. We can't even see that we're in a ditch. It becomes the only life we know.

We believe the LIES.

Believing the lies keeps us stuck. Believing that we're not good enough, that we're a fraud, that we're unlovable, keeps us down in the ditch.

Then we navigate life from deep down in the dark ditch relating to the world from a shame-filled broken heart. We've lost touch with who we really are and tolerate intolerable behavior in others. We don't know we deserve better or that we are worthy of respect and love just because we exist.

We stay put in the ditch because we don't know we're in it. We are stuck in a powerless victim mode.

And worse. We change our goals to meet our behavior or circumstances…instead of adjusting our behavior to meet our goals—like climbing out of the ditch.

I'm just gonna ask—do you WANT to believe these lies?

Do you want to believe that
you're not good enough,
that something's wrong with you
and that you're unlovable?

Because from this moment forward it's up to you.

YOU choose your beliefs. YOU can change your beliefs. YOU can change your behavior.

Beliefs are just thoughts
that we've given a lot of
attention to.

Change your thinking; deliberately think the truth. We'll get to the "how" in another section.

For now, just know YOU can decide to choose what you believe going forward.

FIGHTING FEELINGS

Fighting feelings is hilarious, really. And most of us do it. Daily.

Fighting feelings is like fighting the weather. It's like demanding that the wind *or our guilt* stop, denying that it's raining, *or denying that we feel angry,* or pretending it's sunny when we're in a snowstorm.

No. It's freaking snowing.

Stop lying to yourself.

And, of course, some encourage us into "positive thinking." We can fool ourselves for a bit with this. But, if you put whipped cream on a pile of crap, no matter how sweet you tell me it is, I'm not buying it. Nor am I smelling it.

Just be honest. It's sugar-coated crap.

Better off accepting it for what it is or letting it go.

We can spend our entire lives demanding that the wind stop, denying that it's raining, and pretending that the snow is sun. Exhausting all our efforts, money, and health, lying to ourselves about the reality of the weather. But the reality is, like the weather, feelings are here to stay. As humans we feel. It's part of this deal called life.

NUMB

Many of us pour booze or ice cream into our ditch. We want to mask the loneliness, the shame, the fear, the anger, the sadness. And for a while, this works. We feel better, we feel good, or we simply don't feel.

But then we wonder why we're flat. We lose our zest for life. We lose our inspiration, enthusiasm, joy, and passion.

Numbing out some
of our feelings numbs out all
of our feelings.

We cannot selectively numb....so we're also blocking the passion, joy, and love.

We're flatlining ourselves, making heartgasms near impossible. Then we wonder why we're flat.

Some of us wonder, *Is a flat life worth living?*

Numbing yourself out will
never turn you on.

But numbing yourself can disguise the real issue. Your broken heart.

HOLLYWOOD

Okay, let's talk about you. There's stuff you don't want to feel BUT you also want to feel good.

You want
attention, connection,
and admiration because
it feels like love.
Totally normal.

So you became like a Hollywood actor—at a very young age. You tried on different roles until you got the right part—the one that got you the most attention and love.

You really were a star. Oscar worthy.

You became such a good actor, in fact, that you soon forgot that you were even acting.

You became the role.

You became the full time Miss Perfect, embodied The Hero, ripped it up as The Rebel, dazzled us as Miss Smarty Pants, turned us on as The Seductress or cracked us up as The Comedian...

Meanwhile...

The real you ended up on the cutting room floor.

Rejected.
Abandoned.
Ignored.
Dismissed.

But you were so busy acting that you barely noticed.

Deep down of course, like really deep down, you knew it was an act. Sometimes you even felt it, you felt like a fraud, you felt fake, or suffered from intense loneliness and disconnect.

But this felt like a small sacrifice because a consistent sense of love was flowing in. Plus, you knew how to shut those unwanted feelings up.

THE BLAME GAME

You're numbing out and acting up a storm which gives you the good feels. But the truth is, you've still got a fragile, broken heart underneath it all.

You're still vulnerable.

People behave in ways that create feelings of distress inside you ranging from mild irritation all the way up to full-blown rage. You call this getting triggered.

But if you
look a little closer,
what's really getting triggered
is a sense of not being important,
not being worthy,
or not being
seen.

You secretly fear of course that this is all true…you're petrified that these people might reveal that you really are a fraud and that you're not worthy of love.

You CANNOT risk anyone knowing that you're unlovable. That would be the end of you. You need more protection.

So you develop a bodyguard to make sure that the real you, the one you falsely believe is defective, the one on the cutting room floor, stays down. Your bodyguard keeps the real you hidden. Your bodyguard defends against anyone getting too close and catching a glimpse of the real you. This is done through anger or condemning others.

Rejecting the real you
is what originally broke your heart,
what catapulted you
into acting in exchange
for love.

It's the pain of this heartbreak that kept you acting around the clock in an attempt to feel good.

And you had to act around the clock because the sense of incoming love from the admiration and attention your acting brought didn't last.

You always needed another hit.

And the hit for sure felt good, although part of you could tell it was fake. Because the other actors, the ones providing you a sense of love, were loving your actor; they loved the role you played.

And you were loving their character...neither of you really knew each other.

You were both lost in a movie.

The connection wasn't real.

But the show must go on. You *need* this love. Even if it's not real.

Of course, it felt safe to love this way, the fake way.

If the other actor rejected you or took their love away, it wasn't really *you* being rejected.

It was the role.

But over time,
this fake love brought with it
its own uncomfortable feelings—a
growing sense of isolation,
loneliness, and
misery.

Your bodyguard, oh man, this character was becoming more and more aggressive as the years went on. Anything with a slight hint of rejection or abandonment would trigger your bodyguard's highly developed defensive skills.

But when we're in the blame game, we're stuck in the problem. We're defending our hearts instead of healing them. Sure, if we blame someone when we feel hurt, we can temporarily enjoy a self-righteous buzz. But doing this will never get us what we want.

Bad vibes don't bring good vibes.

Blaming others won't
allow us to feel love.
Neither will blaming
ourselves.

We've got to get out of the vibes of the problem. Protecting our hearts is part of the problem. The solution is on a different level of consciousness. The solution is the vibe of love.

> There is nothing to defend. But there you are, acting, with your lie protected, and you're wondering why you don't feel happy.

And the longer you've been in Hollywood, the messier it gets. Because the pain of rejecting yourself increases. And the cries from the real you on the cutting room floor get louder, making them harder to ignore.

The real you wants to come out, but there's too much to risk. You had to shut that voice up and shut those uncomfortable feelings down.

> The sense of being flawed, the dark belief in your unlovability, were too much to handle. But what can you possibly do from here?

The show HAD to go on.

EXCITEMENT JUNKIE

You noticed right away that excitement, drama, and chaos could blow a thick smoke screen over your heartbreak.

This made you feel better. The buzz of thrill seeking amped you up well above the inner discomfort. The commotion of chaos made it difficult to hear the painful whimpers from the real you.

The drama of *them* was your distraction from *you*.

Maybe you formed a habit of always being late for that buzz of adrenaline you got while rushing from place to place. Or you kept yourself obsessively busy. Believing you were getting things done or crushing it in life—and maybe you were—but you'd also found a clever way to feel high while avoiding any space to experience what was underneath it all, the real you.

You were running at full speed.

Hustling.

Doing, achieving, and shining bright because you thought it'd get you love. But the joke was on you. You cannot run to love. And you cannot outrun yourself.

The only way to get
what you're running after
is to stop running.

But you couldn't stop. The fear was too great.

And those feelings you didn't want to feel kept sprouting up from the *I'm not enough* and *I'm unlovable* rotten soil of shame.

Excitement wasn't enough.
You needed to stop those
feelings.

ADDICTIONS

You started doing drugs. Rails of cocaine shut the feelings up. And you drank.

You ate chocolate and potato chips. You gambled. You sexed. You played mindless games on your phone.

You did
anything that silenced
the voice,
the pain.

You continued acting, while winning accolades and admiration. On the surface, you were enjoying life.

The eating, drugging, and sexing
made you feel fabulous.
For a while.

And people believed you had it all; they envied you. But that was the outside.

That was your act.

Or the addictions made you feel like crap. Which served as a great distraction from the real problem—your belief that something was wrong with you.

One day, it stopped working.

The gambling, the relationships, the food—none of it worked.

The cries were too loud for the booze to drown out.

No amount of time on the internet, watching television, or shopping could shut it up enough.

You were screwed.

Then you had a sudden moment of awareness in which you realized that compulsively doing something to mask the noise would never work.

You could see that it was as silly as blasting music to avoid hearing a jack hammer.

You knew the cries wouldn't stop.

Because it was the TRUTH screaming at you.

You needed to calm the jack hammer. Not distract yourself from it.

So you hit your knees and prayed.

RELATIONSHIPS

Maybe drugs weren't your thing.

Maybe you got off on relationships that didn't work. They got you off of yourself, distracted you from your hidden lie.

Or maybe you got off
on getting off.

You kept dating the same guy. Or gal.

I mean, each lover had a different name. But over and over again, the same type of partner came into your life.

He was emotionally unavailable. You may have noticed this, complained about it to your friends. But did you notice that's part of what made him so hot?

And it made him safe.

Because you could handle the drama.

What you couldn't handle was an emotionally available man getting close enough to you to see the shame your broken heart was drenched in.

Or you dated women who did the push-pull dance. She chased you until you got close, then distanced herself from you.

This gave you a solid dose of distracting drama.

Or your lover was a cheat. Maybe you were. Either way, you were cheating yourself out of any chance of real intimacy.

Because you never showed
who you really were.
How could you?
You weren't showing yourself
the real you, either.

Perhaps you wanted your lover to want you—more than you actually wanted him or her.

Your relationship had enough drama to drown out the truth. You thought it was love. And in a way it was.

You loved being distracted from your buried lie.

At first, the relationship masked the pain perfectly. The honeymoon was pretty sweet. Then it switched, and it seemed your partner was stabbing you in the very part of your heart that was broken—like this person was squeezing lemon in your deepest wound.

> You were left feeling
> more pain than when
> you started going out.

You thought it was your partner's fault.

But all your lover did was illuminate the breaks that were already in your heart.

> You had a choice.
> To wake up and heal
> your heartbreak.
> Or to stay asleep
> and repeat the cycle.

CURTAIN CALL

Some of these strategies worked better than others. You probably had your favorites, the ones that worked best. The ones that silenced the pain and brought you a sense of love.

But if you took the time to get completely honest with yourself, you'd see—you never truly felt loved.

> ### And you weren't happy.
> ### Because it wasn't really you.

It was the actor.

Then, at curtain call, the joke was on you. You suddenly realized you'd been playing a beggar all along.

Begging for attention, affection, and admiration.

> ### Begging for
> ### love.

On top of that, when you went to collect your million-dollar actor's paycheck, you found out that it was YOU who had to pay.

The acting role cost you.

It cost you your truth.
It cost you any chance of real love.
It cost you a piece of
your soul.

But you can end the movie.

You can stop paying those exorbitant and LIFE-stealing prices.

You can step out of the act once you SEE that it's an act.

Because when
you see that the addictions,
the excitement, the dysfunctional
relationships, the constant doing
and not being, the *acting*—that
all of this is what YOU
are buried under,
you can climb
out.

All of this effort is keeping you unhappy and feeling unloved. This is what is keeping you stuck in the ditch.

The stuff you're doing to get love is blocking you from love.

Yikes. Let's get you out of the ditch!

Let's excavate the real you so you can LIVE and LOVE fully.

Let's excavate your heart.

PART TWO:

EXCAVATING YOUR HEART

You are lovable right now.

You can feel love right now. It's in there, under all the barriers you've constructed, underneath all the armor and protection.

It's not outside of you.

Love is not something you can earn. Love is not something you need to prove you're worthy of.

Love is what's inside you, under all that dark, mucky stuff.

This section is designed to guide you in the removal of your barriers to love, the barriers to the real you.

How to Use this Section

The path of the heart is not linear. It's a process. Go through these exercises as you feel called to, in whatever order feels right. You can do them in the order presented, or you can skip over some as you go, coming back to what you skipped later. Or you can use this book as an oracle and do the exercise you flip open to.

Or use this book as kindling, leave it in your doctor's waiting room, add it to your dusty, unread book collection…

BUT if you want LOVE, if you want HAPPINESS, if you want a JOY-FILLED LIFE, you've got to remove what's blocking you from it.

> You've got to *see* how you've been
> blocking yourself from what
> you really want.

Only then can you let the barriers blocking your life force go. And then—nama-f*cking-stay baby—you can enjoy a juicy, multi-heartgasmic life.

A heart exploding with joy, love, passion, and inspiration. A heart FULL of life.

Or you can stay discontent, miserable, and angry. You choose.

BUT promise me this…

Promise me that you'll fondle your heart at least once. Just long enough to experience what happens when you allow it to open and bloom.

Tickle your heart. Let it sing. Even if it's just one song.

Notice
what makes your
heart beat
faster.

You deserve it.

Especially after living in that dark, depressing ditch for decades, running and gunning after a dangling carrot that you will never get to eat.

Come on,
let your heart
flirt with
life.

Try some of these exercises.

*Reminder—Get your free *Heartgasm* bonuses, including guided audios that support the practices in this section, at: kirjohnson.com/heartgasm

YOUR MIND

Getting Your Mind Right

> Thoughts aren't true.
> Mind blowing,
> right?

It's like somehow, we got confused. We believed that just because we think a thought, that it is true. Rather arrogant of our human minds.

Check yourself. Question your thoughts. Examine their truth.

Let's say you notice the thought, *This is going to be hard.*

Is that true? Are you totally sure? How could you possibly know what the future is like?

Okay, maybe you have heaps of experience in which every time you've done a particular thing it was hard. Then ask yourself, *Is this thought helpful? Will it bring me towards my goal?*

Would you be better off dropping the thought and remaining open to the experience?

Believing a thought like, *This is going to be hard,* could easily result in your procrastination, avoidance, or quitting.

It can be that simple.

We think a thought. Then, without examining it, we believe it. This thought continues into a longer, imaginary story. Next, we take action—or don't take action—in accordance with the thought.

So, *It's going to be hard* could lead to not trying.

BOOM. Failure. Based on an unexamined thought.

BUT—what if this is *your dream* that you are blindly thinking that about? Eff that.

You've got to question your thoughts.

You've got to see your train of thinking then check what track that train is on.

> And if the train of thought you're on
> is not headed to the destination
> you want to arrive at—jump
> off the frickin' train!

Jump.

This is the deal. Our beliefs—including the insane *I'm unlovable* or *I'm not good enough* beliefs that are buried deep inside most of us—influence our thoughts.

Our thoughts then inspire our actions. And our actions determine our life experience.

> Belief.
> Thought.
> Action.
> Experience.

This is an ongoing process, but let's keep it simple.

This week, today, or right now, start getting in the habit of questioning the thoughts that are stressing you out.

Like if you notice you're thinking, *I'll never be able to leave this relationship*, pause and ask yourself questions like:

1. Is this thought for sure 100% totally true?

2. Is believing this thought helpful?

3. Will it bring me towards my goal?

4. What am I afraid of?

5. What do I actually want here?

You got this.

And over time,
it will become
more
automatic.

You think, *What if this doesn't work out?* then realize, *This thought isn't helpful, I don't want to be on this thought train,* which leads to choosing a more supportive thought train to ride.

Literally follow that unhelpful thought with something that's helpful like this—*How can I prepare for this to be a success?*

Deliberately get on a thought train
that's heading in the direction
that you actually want to go.

Otherwise, you may keep ending up at the dead-end and life-sucking train station called "I'm unlovable" or "I'm not enough."

Evict the Victim

Most likely, you've got a victim living upstairs. A blaming, criticizing, *why me* complainer who gives power away by believing it's someone else's fault.

STOP.

Stop this grump from hemorrhaging your power. It's not cute. And it just keeps you stuck. Stuck in that freaking ditch.

You evict the victim by moving
responsibility into its place.
You do this by taking
100% responsibility for your life.

This means no blaming. No fault finding. No excuses. You've got to own it, own your life. It's all you. You are your hero. You are your knight in shining armor. You are the one you've been waiting for. You've had the power all along.

Now freaking OWN it.

You are responsible for your thoughts. You are responsible for your feelings. You are responsible for the successes and "failures" in your life. You are responsible for the quality of your relationships. And you are responsible for the direction your life is heading.

Start by dropping the word *can't* from your vocabulary.

Can't is victim lingo. The truth is likely closer to: *I don't want to, I'm not willing to, I'm not available for that, I'm choosing something else…*

It's not that you can't ask him or her out.

It's that you don't want to risk feeling the fear or rejection that asking him or her out could lead to.

It's not that you can't lose weight. Of course you can. It's that you're choosing to spend your time on the couch. Or that you're not willing to give the doughnuts up. Or maybe there is something legitimately in your way like disability or a serious health issue, but you get the point.

We typically have A LOT more power than we tap into.

And it's not that you can't take action towards your dream now. It's that you won't. Or that you're choosing to surrender to fear. Or maybe you're letting your mind entertain untrue stories that discourage you from taking action.

It's incredible what we are willing to settle for instead of risking feeling fear. Demand more for yourself.

Fear is just a feeling. Just little sensations buzzing around inside your body. If you're willing to let that buzz roll through you, then take inspired action, that's called courage.

Acting in alignment with your highest good, despite the fear, yep, that's courage.

Whatever it is that you are saying *can't* about, check it. Know that you CAN. You are probably just choosing not to. Even if you're clever and find an exception to this, just take the point and get that YOU HAVE THE POWER.

You CAN. You totally can.

It's just, will you?!

I dare you. I dare you to choose YOU. I dare you to choose your dream. Be willing to feel what comes up in order to live the life you truly want to live.

I promise you it'll be worth it. And of course YOU are worth it.

And if you really really believe you can't—go back to "Getting Your Mind Right"—are you totally sure you can't? Is that attitude helpful?

Are you willing to flip the script?

Next time you catch yourself thinking that something is happening TO you, become curious.

Ask, *Why is this happening FOR me?*

Because believing that the Universe is conspiring for you or against you is your choice, your decision. Be on your own team.

> Believe what you choose to believe, not what you've been conditioned to believe.

To review:

1. Stop saying *can't.*

2. Stop making excuses.

3. Stop blaming anyone or anything.

4. Contemplate, *Why is this happening for me?*

Notice when you've downshifted into victim gear. Then shift up and out of it.

> Cuz really,
> which gear do you wanna ride in?
> Self pity or self empowerment?
> Moment by moment,
> how you roll is
> your choice.

Shoulding All Over Yourself

Stop shoulding on yourself. Please.

> Should is another word
> I think is best left out
> of our vocabulary.

Should implies rejecting what *is* and carries with it slight criticism for not being where it/we *should* be.

When we say, *I should be further along in my career by now,* or *I should be meditating daily,* or *I shouldn't have eaten that,* we zing ourselves with self condemnation.

Instead of thinking you *should* get outta the ditch—climb out of the ditch! And instead of thinking you *should* be more loving, practice being loving.

Or accept that you're not as loving as you'd like to be right now.

> No need to should all over yourself.

Your self esteem could do without being buried under a pile of shoulds ;)

Waiting for the Future

The future will not be better. Because the future isn't real. We know this in theory; it's living it that gets us.

> Check with yourself—are you
> waiting to be
> happy?

Do you believe that you'll be happy once something happens? Like you'll be happy when you get a promotion, meet a romantic partner, or go on vacation?

This is a great way to stay miserable. Thinking that happiness will happen down the line is a great way to make sure it won't happen now.

This keeps us stuck in the ditch.

I had a friend tell me, *I cannot wait to go on vacation—then I will finally be able to relax and be happy.*

But relaxation and happiness can only happen now. If we choose to think we cannot be happy or relaxed NOW, what makes us think we can be happy and relaxed in the future—which will be experienced as a NOW?

Two months later, she came back from her vacation and told me, "I was stressed out. I tried to relax by the pool but spent the entire time on my phone answering work emails. I fought with my husband the whole time."

The best way to prepare to be relaxed and happy on your vacation in a couple of months is to practice being relaxed and happy now.

Let's try it now with three deep breaths.

Take a deep inhale through the nose. Then exhale through the mouth.

Another deep inhale through your nose. And exhale through your nose.

One more deep inhale. Exhale.

Boom. You are more relaxed.

Taming the Caveman

Back in the cave day, when a saber tooth tiger would come on the scene, your ancestors had a quick choice to make: *Do I eat it or does it eat me?*

And they ran. Or fought. Sadly, those who didn't run or fight have no descendants...

This is known as the stress response, fight or flight, or getting triggered. We've got the same wiring today and when we are in actual danger, it can save our lives.

It's perhaps simplest to think of it like this.

Fear is when we are in actual danger, like there is a physical threat in our environment. Anxiety is imagined danger, a psychological threat.

Both create the same response in our body. Both get us ready to fight or run from the saber tooth tiger.

Perceiving a threat is what triggers us.

Our amygdala—I'll refer to it as our emotional brain— makes that decision quickly in part by bypassing the slower processing neocortex—which I'll refer to as the rational brain.

Fight. Or flight.

Yep, the emotional brain
overrides the rational brain.
Vital for our survival but potentially
harmful for our relationships,
sanity, and health.

Some guy cuts us off in traffic and BOOM we're emo.

Or our girlfriend shows up 10 minutes late for dinner and BAM we're cray.

What's actually triggered is the release of an energizing chemical cocktail, including adrenaline and cortisol.

Your sympathetic nervous system is triggered ON giving your body extra oomph to fight or flee.

And your parasympathetic nervous system is OFF because a cave person doesn't need to digest, rest, or breed when running from that tiger...

We're fired up, without logic, ready
to rage. Even if it was just a text
message that triggered us.

Not cute.

Okay, what to do? You cannot shut off this functioning of your brain, nor would you want to.

But you CAN learn to work with it so that you can be less reactive and speed up your recovery time.

As soon as you notice you're triggered:

1. Count to 10. And if you're super triggered, count to 100. This brings you out of emotional reactivity and into the logical part of your mind where you can choose to respond.

2. Take slow, mindful breaths. This turns on the parasympathetic nervous system. It's simple, just bring your full attention to your nostrils as you inhale slowly. Then exhale. These deep, mindful breaths literally calm your nervous system down.

Here's why you really really want to practice this…

You cannot prevent the dumping of the stress chemical cocktail. What you can do is stop or slow down the dumping once it's started.

When you focus your mind on your breathing or on counting, you are automatically taking your mind off of the STORY that makes your chemical reaction stronger—*He's always late... She has no respect... He's cheating on me... She doesn't love me...*

If you continue entertaining the story with more thoughts, more hazardous chemicals will flood your veins. Then you feel more anxious and amped. Then you'll likely embellish the story with more thoughts. Which dumps more stress chemicals.

This puts you on a downward spiral...

So...get outta the loop as soon as you can. Focus on your breath. Or counting.

Drop the story.

Let yourself calm down back to your loving, amazing, rational self.

Then you can rationally decide what to do or say.

Afterwards, turn on some music and dance. Or go for a run. Let those chemicals sweat out of your body.

You don't want them
inside you.

But if you just let it rip, if you keep swimming in that self-righteous mental story—the stress cocktail buzz can last up to four hours or longer AND leave you hung over.

Irrational and emotionally drained is not a good look on anyone, even you.

Plus, excess stress chemicals lead to serious health issues.

The more you practice this, the more you
will be able to create the life you want
to live—a life lived through response
and choice versus
emotional reaction.

You'll become skilled in separating your thinking and emotions from your actions.

This is super empowering.

Plus, the more you dance outside your comfort zone by trying new things, the more triggered you may be. Or the more fear and anxiety you may face.

If you wanna play BIG, if you want a life filled with love, passion, and happiness—a multi-heartgasmic life— learning how to navigate your triggers is vital.

SELF LOVE

You've been getting your mind right, dropping the act, and responding not reacting—now let's melt into love. Rich, juicy, multi-heartgasmic self love.

You are amazing.

All that acting you started doing when you were little, the roles you took on to get love, it's got to stop.

The *Get Love* thing is backwards.

Acting will only attract other actors and this cannot create authentic love. Because you're loving the role, not the beautiful soul playing the part.

There's no intimacy.
No depth.
It's not real.

Giving love is the answer.

And let's be honest. Acting is begging for love.

You're not a beggar.
You're love worthy just as you are,
without the act, without any need
to do anything other than
just be
you.

Then the question elevates from, *How can I get love* to *Who am I?*

Who's underneath the act of the Hollywood glitz and glamor? Most of us don't know. But you—you are one of the lucky ones who gets to find out.

You GET to discover
who you really are.

You get to drop the act and uncover how amazing you are. And you get to figure out what lights you up. The truth is that your natural, bright light is more attractive than any performance.

We love the truth.

Humans love authenticity. The "me too" or "I'm not alone" factor comforts us. We crave honesty. The vibration of truth hits our body in a deliciously satisfying way.

Take a look at what roles you've taken on. Are you acting perfect? Are you acting bad? Are you acting like you enjoy things you really don't enjoy? Are you acting like you're not angry or sad when you actually are?

Take this week, this day, or this hour to be mindful of what you like and what you don't like.

Start to notice what resonates with you. And notice the dissonance or resistance you feel as you go throughout your day.

Just notice.

Be mindful of when you're acting. Then get real. Drop the act and just be you.

Give us a taste of the raw and real you.

The bonus is that we'll love you for it.

We're craving it.
We crave what's real.
We crave the truth
just like you.

Be Your Own BAE

You've come so far on this journey—you are
AMAZING!

You're well on the path to falling in love with yourself,
lighting up from the inside out, and living a multi-
heartgasmic life. You've already started to become your
own BAE—*Before Anyone Else.*

So beautiful, unique, and wonderful person that you are,
make the commitment. Commit to yourself. Commit
that you come first. Put your oxygen mask on first.

Love yourself first.

This is not selfish—or maybe it is—but in a good way.

You can only give away what you have. So you've gotta
start with self love. Only then can you love others. Keep

discovering who you are, what lights you up, and then shine your light so that others can see it.

This is the practice, honoring yourself, being your own BAE.

Do more of what lights you up.

All the Feels

Feelings get such a bad rap. But why? Let's take a deeper look…

They're entertaining, don't you think? These buzzing waves of energy.

It's like we've got a gang of sensations traveling around inside our bodies. Sometimes they're hot, sometimes cold. They're zipping along or swirling in one spot.

Could it be that simple?

Yet we fear them.
We avoid them.
We deny them.

We poison ourselves in an attempt to silence them.

We fight them off,
defending ourselves against them by
shooting up, drinking, sniffing,
eating, or smoking.

The war continues because everything in our arsenal only temporarily works. But feelings will always win the battle.

Because it is in our nature to feel.

Meanwhile, our compulsive fight
keeps us stuck in a slow suicide.

Why not just surrender?

Energy vibrating
inside our bodies
doesn't have to be that
big of a deal.

And if we want to live a rich life filled with love, joy, and passion—we've got to get good with the feels.

So, what'll it be? Slow suicide and a flatlined life—or do you want to live a multi-heartgasmic life?

Yep, that's what I thought. Let's get juicy.

> # Making peace with our feelings is the path to freedom and the good life.

So then... How do we do it—how do we feel?

1. Drop your attention out of your mind, out of your thinking, and into your body.

2. Notice the sensations buzzing around inside you.

3. Where are the sensations—near your heart, your hands, your legs, your belly?

4. What do they feel like—hot, cold, sharp, big, small, fast, slow?

5. Stay curious to what's happening inside your body. Continue letting go of your thoughts, dropping any story, by bringing your attention to the sensations in your body.

It's that simple.

When we feel the feelings, they can pass through us.

When we jump on a thought train, a long, drawn-out story that generates more feelings, we can stay stuck in an intense feeling—for minutes, days, or decades.

The more we think about it, the more we feel about it. And the more we feel about it, the more we think about it.

We get caught in a loop, lost in the story.

The way out is presence.

Just feel.

Practice dropping your attention
out of your mind and
into your body.

Let the energy of the feels flow through you.

You may even discover a richness in the sensations you call sadness, anger, or jealousy.

That's right,
you may find yourself
in awe of the wonderful,
internal experience of
buzzing sensations.

You don't have to get swept up in the storm, you can witness the beauty as it blows through.

And really, feelings are only a big deal when we try to fight them.

Mental Tsunamis

Okay, so feel.
But what about
the BIG ones?
you ask…

I call these "mental tsunamis." It's like we get hit with a tidal wave of rage or disgust, a whirlpool of sadness or grief, or smacked around in a storm of doubt.

Then what? What do we do when the big ones come?

Same same.

Imagine you're in the ocean during a tsunami. The only way to avoid getting pummeled by the massive wave is if you dive deep into the ocean.

> We do the
> same during intense emotions.
> We dive our attention
> deep into our
> bodies.

The mental tsunami is only dangerous if we stay up in our heads where our thinking is.

So we must stop thinking about whatever is triggering the emotion—the situation, the story, the person—by diving our attention into the calm water, the sensations in our body.

The alternative is getting swept away in the emotional storm, staying reactive to life, and being tossed on shore wherever and whenever the mental storm decides to spit you out.

Or you could use addictions to numb out the tsunamis for a decade or two until you are slammed onto your knees.

Assuming you survive the addictions.

The next time you notice that you're in a mental tsunami, stay curious, detached, and safe by diving deep.

Then transmute the feeling and emerge free.

Here's how:

1. Notice the sensations. Where in your body is the "loudest" or most intense energy or feeling? Your gut, chest, throat or...??

2. Check the size of the "loud" sensation. About how big is it? Would you say it's about the size of a basketball, apple, grape or...?

3. Take a breath.

4. Check again. How big is it now? Did it change in size?

Every time I've guided a client through this or checked myself—whether it's an anxiety attack, anger, doubt, guilt or grief—the sensations are smaller on the double check.

Boom.

This is your new SUPER POWER.

Experiencing how our consciousness changes matter—how our attention affects the sensations, especially in a matter of seconds, and in a way that we prefer, meaning the feeling lessens in intensity—is life changing.

Because it takes us from feeling highly emotional, overwhelmed, and lost in a story of victimhood to the empowered seat of choice in how we respond with the external world, meaning we can create and shape shift our future in real time.

This is everything.

You Are Not Your Feelings

You are not your feelings; give 'em some space.

Call them out for what they are.

Instead of feeling sadness and jumping on a thought train into Sad Storyville, say to yourself, *Sadness is here.* And then let the sadness wash through you. Notice the sadness without getting lost in it, without taking it personally.

> Bring your A-game to
> nonjudgmental awareness.

Sadness is here.

If you judge it by thinking, *This is bad... I will always be depressed... I don't like feeling sad... This means something...*just notice that you are judging. Then see if you can go back to curiosity without judging the judging.

Back to *Sadness is here.*

It doesn't have to mean something. Mind blowing—right?!

Witness and allow the sadness
without identifying with it.

Next time fear arises, notice it.

Greet it with, *Oh, hi Fear, you're here.*

Creating a story or adding TIME
to the feeling isn't necessary.

And probably not helpful.

Time is where our suffering is. The time dimension
sounds like, *And it will always be this way* or *This ruined my
whole year.*

Think about it.

All we have is THIS moment.
The one right NOW.

The only way to RUIN
this moment is to add
time to it.

Because if, in this moment, you are thinking that your whole year was ruined—it's actually THIS specific thought that is ruining THIS moment.

This is life changing. Maybe reread the last short paragraph.

You can choose to drop TIME any time.

We drop time
by becoming
present.

Here's how.

Focus on your breath, on experiencing the world through your senses, or by dropping your attention into the sensations in your body.

This is part of accepting yourself.

Allowing
your emotions to flow
through you is a
big part of
self love.

Cancelling the Guilt Trip

A lot of us were guilted as children by well-meaning parents who used guilt to get us to behave in a desired way. The problem now is that we continue to allow guilt to drive our behavior.

> It's as if we leave our house in the morning, jump in the back seat of our life, buckle up, and allow guilt to drive us around all day.

Sometimes this is called people pleasing.

The way out is stupid simple. Feel the feels. Then consciously choose your next move.

Because here's the deal.

> Just because you're invited on a guilt trip, doesn't mean you have to attend.

You can get free from being guilted.

The price tag
is your willingness and ability
to notice the sensations of guilt without
allowing the avoidance of it to
dictate your behavior.

This was a radical shift for me, when at five years sober, I was feeling guilt on a silent meditation retreat for the first time.

I mean literally, like allowing myself to feel the guilt, without trying to make it go away.

I'd snuck out of the meditation center in Chiang Mai, Thailand, in search of food. Halfway around the mountain, I changed my required white meditation clothes for colored clothes. God forbid I stay in the white clothes and get spotted as an escaped meditator...Yea, my mind went there.

I was hungry and bought two big waffles to "cope" with the fact that we weren't allowed to eat after noon.

While walking back to the meditation center, I felt tremendous guilt.

It was a new experience—to notice
the guilt and to allow it
to be.

It blew me away that I didn't "know" guilt. That I'd never actually felt it before, like I'd allowed myself to be manipulated by others so that I could avoid feeling the buzz called guilt.

I declared right there, with one hand on a waffle and one hand on my bag of white meditation clothes, that I'd never again let guilt control me.

I vowed to allow the sensation we call "guilt" to be in my body while I choose how I want to behave.

This is freedom…
when we notice our thoughts,
notice our feels
and CHOOSE how we
want to engage with
the moment.

So next time you notice you're invited on a guilt trip, you know what to do.

1. Drop your attention into your body.

2. Feel the buzz of the sensations we call "guilt."

3. Decide how you want to respond.

These days, when I'm invited on a guilt trip, my inner world has a new reaction.

I notice that it's happening, that someone is attempting to use guilt to coerce me, and instead of feeling guilt, I feel compassion.

Because
I imagine the soul wanting to
bring me on a guilt trip is using guilt
because they have also been
manipulated through
guilt in their past.

This is sad. And because I can see it now, my heart opens. So yea, compassion.

And then BOUNDARIES.

Bon voyage, guilt trips.

Getting Your Shame Off

Guilt says *What you did was wrong*. Shame says *You are wrong*. Shame says *You're not good enough*. Shame says *You're unlovable*.

Shame is a dirty lie buried deep in
your subconscious mind
that whispers,
Something's wrong with you.

Shame oozes its tar-like toxicity up into your thinking, discouraging you and crushing your spirit. Then these shame-tainted thoughts direct the actions you take—and the actions you don't take.

Shame drives your life.

And the shame's not even yours.

You did not, on your own and without influence, decide one day that you're unlovable or that something's wrong with you.

That'd be insane.

When you were little, shame stemmed from your parents, teachers, siblings—from people who'd already been shamed themselves.

> When you
> believed the lies of shame,
> you took the shame on.

You believed that you're unworthy of love as you are.

This is madness.

> The *I'm unlovable* belief is
> perhaps the greatest lie ever told.
> Believing it is traumatic.
> It's heartbreaking.
> Literally.

When we believe we are unlovable, and a lot of us do, we bury that belief and the emotional pain it causes deep inside.

Let's dig that sucker up! Let's get your shame off.

1. Recognize it's a lie.

2. Get honest—see that you've got this lie buried inside you.

3. Dive into your unresolved grief and *feeeeeeeel* it.

> It's the grief
> buried in our hearts
> that needs to be healed.
> This enables us to return to love.

We start by grieving that we could believe the unbelievable—that something is wrong with us and that we are therefore unlovable. We may find deep healing in grieving the specific things that we were told and the way we were treated that inspired us to believe the shame-filled lies in the first place.

Then comes the grieving for the people who convinced us of these lies.

> Because after we grieve for our
> own pain, we can see that they too,
> deep down believe the same things
> about themselves.

And this is also heartbreaking.

I know, I know, it sounds like a lot. And it is. But trying to get love or proving your lovability is as silly as a fish trying to run or a bird trying to ride a bike.

It's just frickin' wrong.

YOU ALREADY ARE LOVABLE.

> Nothing is wrong with you.
> You are totally worthy of love.
> Especially your own.

It's time to excavate the toxic shame from your heart. Healing your shame requires absolute self love in the form of radical acceptance.

This means accepting and allowing all of the feelings you've previously rejected.

> Feelings are energy; they didn't just disappear because you didn't want to feel them.

The affirmations *I am lovable* and *I accept myself* can help. Try them.

Keep saying them until you believe them.

Every day and throughout the day, *I love and accept myself.*

> When you
> reach that deep place
> of absolute conviction—the
> *I refuse to reject myself any longer* place,
> you are ready to heal
> your toxic shame.

It may take a bit of time to get to that resolve. Or maybe you're already there.

BUT when you are there—when you absolutely 100% refuse to reject yourself—that is radical self love.

That is the place from which you can heal your shame.

That is the attitude that opens you up to the deep healing of your heart.

> Because when you refuse
> to reject, abandon, or ignore
> yourself anymore, you
> are open to love.

You are open to allowing, accepting, and loving yourself so deeply that it's a no brainer to heal the lies.

To let them go.

To feel your way through everything you had previously trapped inside.

> We feel our way
> to freedom.

I did this deep healing work on my own over four months. I was completely committed to healing my heart—to loving myself. I grieved daily—crying for a couple minutes or up to a couple hours.

It was the most loving time of my life.

> But to be clear, this isn't
> just crying. This is what I call
> CONSCIOUS GRIEVING—
> using the techniques we already
> discussed on how to feel and
> transmute emotions.

Here's what I mean.

If a thought comes, like *Mommy or Daddy didn't love me*, notice the story. Allow the emotions that arise to rise, then drop the thought. Ditch the story completely, then dive down into the sensations of grief.

Perhaps there's a lump in your throat, tears coming to your eyes, or tightness in your chest.

If you notice a lump in your throat, become curious and detached; do not want it to be any different than it is.

> No resistance,
> no avoidance,
> no agenda
> except to notice it.

Gauge the size of the "lump." Keep your attention on the sensations without adding time or mental stories, even if there is truth to the stories—drop 'em.

> This is the essence of
> self love—radical acceptance
> of what IS.

Allowing our inner world to be as it is. The interesting thing is…when we are able to do this, to accept ourselves exactly as we are in the moment, our inner world transforms.

It's as if all we need
is our own love.

This is why the conscious grieving journey was a super loving time for me…because it was the first time that I had ever truly allowed my inner world to be exactly as it was while meeting it with my full attention, my loving presence.

While you can do this healing alone, I'd recommend getting support. Perhaps a therapist or spiritual mentor.

I promise you, this is the journey of a lifetime, the journey of releasing the shame-filled lies.

It's the
journey from living
in your head
to living from
your heart.

Own Your Humanity

You're gonna flop. You'll fail, get rejected, stumble, and flash your imperfections.

This is normal. This is reality. Own it, own your humanity.

> All of life can be
> viewed as learning.

From this perspective, failure doesn't exist. We try something and either get closer to or further from our desired outcome.

We either hit the target or we need to try again.

No need to have intense feelings about trying again. Although if they come, by all means, feel those bad boys! Notice them blow through your body. Allow them. And then gather the data of what works, what doesn't, and keep on keeping on.

Becoming aware of your limitations is what allows you to break through them.

What if you're exactly where you're supposed to be, learning the exact lesson at the exact time that you are meant to?

What if the challenge you're facing—and the learning you can gain from it—are for your highest good, for the evolution of your soul?

What if it can ultimately bring you closer to your goal? This has been my experience. That the "worst" things, like having alcohol ripped from my life, turn out to be the best things, like being sober.

> After all,
> it's called a life BEYOND
> our wildest dreams because we
> CANNOT see it now,
> it's beyond our
> vision.

And so maybe, just maybe, the "tragedies" or our "failures" of today are the required circumstances to move us beyond our current life and rocket us into one beyond our wildest dreams.

STOP Rejecting Yourself

Stop abandoning yourself.

> It's a violent act to ignore, deny,
> or reject your feelings.

It's rejecting yourself.

No need to lie to yourself anymore. You can be on your team now.

If you feel sad, be sad. If you feel angry, let it rip; at least internally, notice it's there.

Give space to what's happening, allow it, accept it.

> Refuse to
> reject what's happening
> in your internal
> world.

Love yourself enough to let it be.

Take note throughout your day to when you are rejecting or abandoning yourself. What boundaries are you allowing to be crossed? When are you not speaking up for yourself? Where are you pretending to feel different than you do? When are you allowing yourself to be treated in a way that is unacceptable to you?

> Commit to
> no longer rejecting yourself.
> This is a radical act. You can
> totally choose to do it.
> This is love.

Total Acceptance

Perhaps the most important ingredient to loving ourselves and loving others is acceptance. We're talking total and complete acceptance. If we continue to reject parts of ourselves, we will reject parts of others.

Let's keep it simple.

> Moment by moment,
> notice if you are rejecting
> or accepting yourself.

Are you allowing your feelings? Are you being honest with yourself? Yes, we kinda just discussed this. But it may be helpful to consider both as you go through your day—refusing to reject yourself and radically accepting yourself.

Accepting ourselves doesn't mean we launch a revolution.

We can accept that we feel something or want to change something but don't necessarily have to take action.

You can start by accepting (believing) the truth which is—you are enough and you are lovable.
Affirm it.

> Like literally say throughout the day,
> *I am lovable. I am good enough.*
> *I accept myself.*

Yesing Yourself

Acting is no-ing yourself. It's self rejection.

Screw that.

Even when acting gets you love, you will likely later resent that you no-ed yourself. Yes yourself.

Say yes to what is happening with you right now.
Yes to where you are right now.
Yes to how amazing you are right now.
Yes you are enough.
Yes you are lovable.
Yes right now
YES.

The mind can tell us we *should* be different than we are, further along than we are, more mature than we are, wealthier than we are, more loving than we are…

but that's not real.

That's a mind game that invites your critic to judge the crap out of you.

Just say yes. Yes to what is.

Yes, right now I am scared. Yes, right now I am greedy. Yes, right now I just yelled at someone who cut me off in traffic.

Yes doesn't mean and *I'm proud of it, I endorse it,* or *I condone it.* It just means YES, this is happening right now.

You are yesing reality.

Once I had an anxiety attack while sitting at my desk at work, freaked out, grabbed my phone, and ran outside. It was lunch time and I was in the South of Market area in San Francisco. I called a friend while crying near one of the busy South Park restaurants. I said to her, "I can't believe this. Am I really 35 years old crying on my lunch break in a crowded park and with no clue what started the anxiety?"

She replied, "Yes! Yes, that is exactly what's happening right now." Then I laughed. Because she was right.

Her simple words guided me to accept reality.

If I had stayed in *This should not be happening,* or *I'm too old for this,* or *I will always be this way,* I would have stayed stuck. Judging myself would have inspired more intense emotions only to amplify the situation. Plus these thoughts, these judgments, and *shoulds* aren't true.

If I allowed myself to believe them, I would have been using the illusion of time to make myself feel worse.

Think about it.

Here's the dimension of time again. It's important to understand, which is why I'm bringing it up a second time.

> Time is where our suffering lies—our suffering is in the story we make up about something that includes the time dimension.

And yesing—accepting reality—doesn't mean we stay there.

So maybe it's *Yes, I got stuck in a ditch* and also *Yes, I'm going to do everything in my power to change this situation.*

We don't resign to staying in the ditch.

We just acknowledge what's actually happening.
Yes, I'm in a ditch, panicking and crying on my lunch break. And yes, I will do what I can to move through this.

I will continue to meditate, practice mindfulness, journal my feelings—do the things that reduce my anxiety while rewiring my brain. Yes, I will climb out of this ditch.

> Drop time,
> drop the story, and
> YES the reality of
> this moment.

Say yes to the life flowing through you. Say yes to curiosity. Say yes to you.

You *should* not be different than you are right now. Yes yourself. Right now. Go ahead, nobody is looking.

YES!

Make Love to Yourself

Take a deep breath.

Inhale. Exhale.

Now calmly walk to a mirror.

And, for a full minute, look deep in your eyes and say, *I love you. I love you. I love you…*

Fully accept whatever comes.

Tears.
Laughter.
Smiles.
Grief.
Accept it all.
Let the judgment go.

I love you. I love you. I love you.

Do this every day until it feels good.

I love you.
I love you.
I love you.

Then do it some more.

You are so lovable.
Do you see it?

Bathroom Quickie

When you notice that you're triggered or you are feeling unloved, skip to the loo.

Take five minutes in the
bathroom to come back to you,
to come back to the truth.

Come back to love.

Place one hand on your heart and start taking slow, deep breaths. This will literally change the chemical process happening inside your beautiful bod and calm you down. Oxytocin—a trigger antidote—will be released.

Imagine you are breathing in and out of your heart.

Visualize a calm,
white energy coming inside
your heart, then exhale it out.

Try closing your eyes while you do this. Keep your hand on your heart and visualize the calm coming in.

Continue this heart breathing for a couple of minutes, soothing yourself in this bathroom quickie.

Once you feel a bit calm, you can add in some gratitude.

With your hand still on your heart, bring to mind three things you're grateful for. Visualize the first one, then connect with the feeling. Feel the gratitude in your heart for this wonderful thing. Then say *Thank you* and move on to the next one.

Over time, we get better at soothing ourselves and softening our triggers. This is what we are going for.

> There's no freedom
> in fighting or resisting
> those who push our buttons—
> it's better to remove our buttons
> so that there's no buttons
> to be pushed.

The solid work you are doing from this book will help you get free.

Trigger by trigger, we wire our nervous system back to peace.

Making Love

Making love is a great daily practice.
Making love in our own hearts,
that is.

Here we are cultivating the love inside our heart and then showering ourselves with it.
Let's ease right into the love making.

Place your hand on your heart. Bring your attention into your heart space.

Imagine that you are breathing in and out of your heart. Take slow and deep breaths. Aim to inhale and exhale for three to four times longer than normal.

When you begin thinking, gently bring your attention back to your heart.

Closing your eyes can help you concentrate on your heart.

Now bring to mind a time
when you felt loved.

Maybe this was with a specific person, with your pet, or in nature. Visualize that experience then bring the feeling of connectedness and love to the current moment.

Continue the deep breathing while recalling the love. Bathe in it, shower in the love. Keep showering in the love for as long as you wish.

> Anytime
> you feel like
> you need
> a little love,
> make love with
> yourself.

And just like how the more often you work out your bicep, the stronger it gets—the more love making you do with your heart, the greater your heart's capacity for love grows.

You got this.

> Everything
> you need is
> inside
> you.

Keeping the Vibe Alive

Keep your vibe alive. Seriously, is there anything worth shutting down your life force for? Think about it.

But we do it all the time.

We experience something we don't like and we close our hearts.

> We think we are protecting ourselves. What we are actually doing is closing off the life force flowing though us.

Then we suffer from the depleted energy, from the closed-down life force.

> Staying open is easier than opening back up.

So this is where we start.

We practice staying open to life, keeping our hearts open regardless of what happens.

Notice when you're open and notice when you're closed.

See if you can
notice when you
close down.

Closing down may include thoughts like, *This is annoying,
I don't want to be here, This is wrong,* or any thoughts about
wanting the reality of the moment to be different.

Resisting the moment—which is
resisting life—can result in our
hearts closing
down.

When you notice you are closing down, drop your
attention into your heart while having an intention to
stay open to what is happening.

Say yes to the experience. See if you can let whatever it
is you're experiencing move through you while you stay
open.

When you get triggered,
practice staying
open.

To be clear, yesing life does not mean accepting abuse. You may yes yourself and also say yes to having boundaries while walking away from a situation.

It follows that when we feel a no inside, we say no.

No, I don't want to use my limited funds for that trip. No, I don't want to get a matching tattoo with you. No, I don't want a drink.

Trust the energy flowing inside you. Trust the no's.

The key here
is staying open
regardless of what's
happening.

Like saying no to a request while saying yes to the reality of the moment.

Yes, she or he asked me out. No, I don't want to accept. Yes, I am accepting that this is happening. Yes, I will stay open to the moment while having boundaries that honor myself.

We tend to shut our hearts when we find something unacceptable. Notice this.

Notice if you're shutting down your life force with your judgements.

Even if you are right.

Notice how it feels to judge and shut down.

What good is being right when it shuts you off from your own life force?

Stay open.

The more rules we have about how life is to be, the more we are setting ourselves up to get triggered and potentially shut down.

This week, today, or for the next hour, notice how your thoughts and the life force flowing through you are related.

Keep your energy, your vibe, alive.

Give Trees a Chance

Now let's "yes" some nature. Go to the woods, a park, or outside where there's a tree.

Meditate with the tree.

Sit in front of it. Touch it. Stare at it. Better yet, lay underneath it and look up at it. Throw down a blanket. Then lay back, soak up the good vibes Earth emits, and take in the tree.

Spend at least 15 minutes with the tree. Just look at it. See if you can feel it, if you have any emotional reaction when connecting with the tree. Commune with it. Allow the tree to guide you back to your own nature.

Ask it questions. Like the deep ones you have about life. Then listen.

An hour with a tree can be life changing.

You do not want to miss this one. Seriously, give trees a chance.

YOUR BODY

Roll It Out

All those emotions we didn't feel—the ones we poured booze, sex, and ice cream over, the emotions we blocked with social media, TV marathons, or gambling—they didn't just disappear.

They got locked down inside our body.

And part of our healing journey—part of getting free and living a multi-heartgasmic life—is releasing the old emotions.

Myofascial release is great for this.

The unfelt emotions from our past can get stored deep inside our fascia. Fascia is the connective tissue that covers our muscles, tendons, ligaments, and organs. Think of it like a giant spider web inside our body. When we get a knot at one part of it, it pulls on the rest of it. And because of this, we may have a knot in our shoulder yet we feel pain in our knee. No worries, let's release the old emotions.

Foam rollers are great. So is using two tennis balls. I prefer the two rubber balls (slightly harder than tennis balls) that I got at a yoga studio that are specifically designed for myofascial release. When we lay on the balls or foam roller for half a minute or longer, we can start to feel the knot release.

Emotion may release as well. Tears may fall or a memory may surface. This will also release tension.

Release the emotions and get free.

Here's how. Lay on the ground, put the balls under your shoulder blades, ribs, back, butt…

You'll know you've got the balls in the right place because the knots, the trigger points, will feel a bit painful when the balls are pressed into them. Breathe and hold until you feel the release.

This works the same for a foam roller. Put the roller under your spine and perpendicular to your body. Then slowly roll your spine across the roller while pausing for at least 30 seconds on each spot that feels slightly painful.

You'll likely know when it's time to move because you'll feel the release.

Shake & Chill

Working out is another great and super fun way to free old emotion or energy from the body.

When our bodies don't move, they stagnate.

So babe, shake that thang.

Try this 30-minute workout recipe. Turn music on for the first 20 minutes.

Set a timer and have fun.

1. 10 minutes of body shaking: Keep your feet firmly on ground and shake your shoulders up and down. Then add a bounce to your shoulder shake by bending your knees.

2. 10 minutes of dancing: Then let it flow, dance dance dance in any way your body wants to move.

3. 10 minutes of sitting down: Close your eyes and focus on your breath.

This is especially good if you have a fairly active mind. The movement can help to clear away excess mental noise before you sit down to meditate.

Smiling on the Inside

Everything is connected. Negative thinking leads to a negative mood which sends bad vibes throughout our body.

Turn up the good vibes. We can do this by smiling at our insides. I know, I know—try to suspend your judgement and just give it a whirl.

1. Sit down on the floor or chair with an upright spine.

2. Set timer for 5-20 minutes.

3. Close your eyes and take five slow, mindful breaths.

Smile.

Imagine sending that smile, that loving, warm energy, to your heart. Talk to your heart, thank it for all it does for you. Thank it for sending your body fresh blood and nutrients, for communicating to you when you like someone or something, and whatever else you'd like to appreciate your heart for.

Now send that smile to your lungs. Express your gratitude to your lungs for all that they do.

Then send the smile to your kidneys. Thank your kidneys.

Next send that love to your liver. Thank your liver.

Keep sending your loving smile inward.

Next bring the loving smile to your stomach.

Continue sending the smile around, connecting with your organs, and blessing them with heaps of good vibes.

LOVING OTHERS

Bombing the Barriers

When we feel that we're lacking love in our lives, it's likely that our heart is blocked.

Most of us have these barriers to love—but no worries, they are removable.

You built them up AND you can certainly tear them down.

These next couple of practices are
like throwing a grenade
at the steel walls of
your heart.

And you might feel like you've been bombed—at least at first.

The path
to love doesn't
always feel like love.
It often feels
like all the old
emotions that you
tried not to feel.

Like when you drank over getting fired. Or found a quick rebound after a breakup. Or all the childhood pain you minimized and shoved down.

That energy needs to be released in order to get free.

These bombs can shatter and destroy that old pain.

They can free your heart.

It's obviously up to you if you wanna stay blocked from love.

It's your heart—you've gotta decide if you wanna stay love lacking or if you wanna free that baby from the bitterness, judgement, and arrogance it's been hiding behind.

The real question of this
book is this—do you want to
live a
multi-heartgasmic,
vibrant life
or do you want to
flatline and
feel dead
inside?

Choose love.

Loving the Kindness

This practice is from a Buddhist meditation called Metta or Loving Kindness.

You are releasing your barriers to love when you nonjudgmentally allow your grief, anger, or sadness during Metta. That is the healing taking place.

> These
> are exactly the spots
> over your heart where you've
> been blocked from
> love.

And through witnessing your emotions—through noticing the feelings without entertaining any thoughts that arise—you are returning to love.

In Metta, we repeat specific phrases in our mind.

When intense emotions come, drop the phrases and switch to mindfulness by noticing the sensations in your body. Then, when the emotion passes, pick the phrases back up.

We start offering these phrases to ourselves. Sit comfortably and close your eyes. Bring to mind an image of yourself.

Repeat each of these phrases one by one while connecting with your heart's desire for yourself to be happy, safe, strong, at peace:

> May I be happy
>
> May I be safe
>
> May I be healthy and strong
>
> May I be at peace and at ease

Continue these phrases with yourself in mind for a couple of minutes.

Next, switch to a loved one.

Bring an image of a loved one to mind. Repeat each phrase in your mind. *May you be happy. May you be safe. May you be healthy and strong. May you be at peace and at ease...*while connecting with the sentiment, your desire for your loved one to be happy. Feelings of warmth, friendliness, or love may arise. Just notice it all without creating any stories or getting lost in thought. Continue this for a couple of minutes.

Next, switch to a neutral person.

This is someone you don't have strong positive or negative feelings towards—it's not a friend or someone you're in conflict with. This may be someone you've overlooked, been too busy to connect with, or ignored because it's just not possible to emotionally engage with everyone. Like the new barista at your local cafe, the man whom you dropped your dry cleaning off to this week, or the woman who you see at the gym sometimes but have no real feelings towards.

Send them the Metta wishes while holding an image of them in your mind for a couple more minutes. *May you be happy. May you be safe. May you be healthy and strong. May you be at peace and at ease…*

Now switch to a difficult person. Someone whom you have conflict with. This could be the office bully, a stranger like a celebrity or politician, your partner, or your mom.

Visualize the difficult person in your mind's eye and send them the loving kindness wishes. If strong emotions come, pause and notice the emotions. Drop out of any story created through your thinking and just notice what happens in your body.

Continue with the difficult person for a couple of minutes as long as it doesn't get overwhelming.

Lastly, we visualize all beings. Send the phrases to all of humanity, to all animals, and to the entire world.

If you really want to free your heart—rinse, repeat.

> You can practice
> Metta daily to burn the hatred,
> judgment, and "negative" emotions
> from your
> heart.

You probably noticed that the difficult person is actually someone whom it's difficult for you to love.

> They are
> your gurus—because
> they show you
> exactly where you
> are blocked from love.

May you be at peace.

Provoking Compassion

Typically, we humans shut down our hearts because the emotional pain is severe. Or so we feel at the time. But how open do you want your heart to be?

How much of your life force do you want access to?

Are you willing to breath in the pain of others or even the pain of the world?

A life changing question to consider is, *How free do you want to be?*

Being totally open and free includes our willingness to get touched by our own and other peoples' suffering.

Tonglen is a Tibetan Buddhist practice where we do exactly this—where we open our hearts to the suffering of others and respond with care, compassion, or joy.

In Tonglen, we breathe in suffering and exhale compassion or joy.

Start by bringing to mind a specific type of suffering. Like people dying of cancer, starving children, or the suffering of the homeless.

Now sit in an upright, comfortable position and close your eyes. Take a couple of mindful breaths.

Imagine the suffering of these people.

Visualize it as black smoke. When you inhale, breathe this black smoke of their suffering into your heart. Briefly pause. Then as you exhale, visualize white light coming out of your heart while you send these suffering people compassion and ease from their suffering or even joy.

Continue breathing this way for fifteen minutes, inhaling suffering and exhaling relief.

Our egos may find this practice extremely provocative— it may trigger strong feelings causing us to resist even trying it. Our minds might say, *Why would I want to bring imaginary suffering into my heart?* or *But what about keeping my vibration high?*

At least this is what I thought at first... It took me a couple of days on the retreat where I learned this before I could actually do it. I sat there in the meditation hall in Katmandu, Nepal, where we were guided to practice

Tonglen, and only focused on my breath. I refused. My ego did not want to imagine black smoke coming into my body, let alone my heart—until it became real.

> My willingness
> began the moment
> I witnessed someone on the
> retreat actually suffering.

I happened to be assisting a nun on that retreat in Nepal. A few days into the retreat, she had an accident and told me about it. I immediately hit my cushion in the meditation hall, breathed in the *black smoke* of her suffering, and sent her compassion, care, and a healing white light.

Keep this as a powerful tool in your toolbox for when you encounter suffering in your environment. It's likely all around you.

> We are not
> taking on the burdens
> of the world with
> Tonglen.

We're acknowledging the suffering of others and accepting it. In doing this, we are transforming our hearts.

The world is changed one heart at a time.

And so we start with ours.

Love Generation

Many of us hold disappointment, sadness, anger, or even rage and hatred in our hearts towards our family members.

This keeps us locked inside a closed-down heart.

We can get free.

Understanding is a good place to begin. Let's start with our parents. When we try to understand why they may have acted the way they did—or didn't—forgiveness is possible.

It's helpful
to think of forgiveness as
no longer letting the past block our
hearts from present-day
love.

Forgiveness is certainly not condoning or approving anyone else's behavior.

Sit in a comfortable, upright seated position. Bring to mind some of your own suffering.

Maybe your dad never told you he loved you. Or your mom was drunk and emotionally unavailable during your childhood.

Or you were adopted, the middle child, moved around a lot, or were even abused in some way. Just start by considering your childhood suffering and notice the first grievance that comes to mind.

Whatever the grievance is, go into it.
Go into the "pain," the sensations
inside your body that arise,
when you think of what
your parents did
or did not do.

Do this one parent at a time.

Let the tears flow. Feel what you were unwilling to feel before.

If the pain is particularly deep, or there was abuse, you may want to do this under the care of a therapist. There is tremendous healing that takes place when you're in the presence of an empathetic guide. And you may feel safer to go deep into your pain with a trained professional there.

Back to the grievance. Maybe you felt betrayed, rejected, or unimportant.

> Underneath most of the grievances
> is a sense of not being
> good enough or not
> being loved.

Feel what that feels like. Of course, use your intuition and if it becomes overwhelming, back off.

At a certain point, the energy will likely shift. You may feel it change and notice that the tears slow and the emotional storm passes. This may not happen the first time you go into a specific grievance, particularly if the pain runs deep.

But consider this. For each time we shoved down our feelings, that emotion got lodged inside our body. To heal, we need to release that emotion. It's energy.

Let's imagine that each unfelt grievance from your past is an energetic marble stored on top of your heart. These marbles are blocking your life force and your ability to love. They are filled with the emotions you previously refused to feel.

Let's continue to imagine that you had 100 painful experiences that you tried to ignore or reject. Then your healing work would include bringing to mind the specific grievances and feeling them.

This likely means crying.

Conscious grieving frees us from our past.

Again, here's how we do it—when the feels come, drop your thoughts. Notice the sensations that arise from the past hurt with your full attention. This allows each marble, each old grievance, to be released from your heart.

As you continue to release the old emotion, your heart opens and your ability to love returns. How rad is that?!

You will probably notice when the marble is gone because there is a shift in energy (you may notice it lose its potency or strength). At that point, we may want to focus on who "caused" the grievance.

We do this so that we can live FREE.

Let's say your dad never said he loved you and you were just feeling the pain of that heart wound. When you feel the shift in emotional energy, think of your dad with a slight detachment.

Consider how sad it is that a man could not tell his own child these simple yet important words, *I love you*.

Use your own experience—your "wounds"—when you do this. Consider what may have happened or did not happen to him as a young boy. *Did his parents not openly share love with him? Did he never feel good enough?*

Consider the sadness he may have felt in his own childhood that caused him to lock his heart behind steel walls.

We can only
give what we have—
we do what we know.

If we weren't raised with unconditional love, and most of us weren't, it would be difficult to fully accept our babies when we become parents. A sane and emotionally healthy parent would not intentionally harm their child.

Imagine what that little boy, your dad, might have felt. See him as a child who also didn't feel loved. Feel what it feels like to see your own dad wounded at that young age.

One way forgiveness can start is when we understand that our parents may have done their best. They did what they knew.

They reacted with the
level of consciousness
that they had
at the time
we felt harmed.

Tears may come when considering what your dad, as a little boy, may have experienced or felt.

Go into it.

After that emotion dissipates, move to his parents. Your grandparents could only have raised your father with what they knew.

Continue the grieving process.

Consider your great-grandparents as children.

Then consider all parents.

Extend your grieving out to all people who caused harm to their children and feel that pain.

You are grieving
the pain of the world.
You are blowing your
heart wide open.
You are becoming
multi-heartgasmic.

You are getting free.

Little Parents

Close your eyes. Imagine your mom as a little girl. See her, in your mind's eye, running up to you full of spontaneity, happiness, and joy. She gives you a big hug and sits next to you. She tells you her dreams, her hopes, her fears. She tells you what she wants to be and do when she's older.

With a shy smile, she even tells you that she wants to be a mother. Sit with her.

> Feel her exuberant spirit,
> her zest for life.

Now do the same with your dad. Imagine him as a little boy. He's full of life and comes towards you. He shares with you his dreams, his hopes, and his fears. He hugs you and then looks in your eyes.

He tells you that one day he wants to be a father. Seeing our parents as innocent children and hearing their desires to have babies can be incredibly transformative. Go into it.

You can even imagine what they hoped for you when you were first born.

PART THREE:

COME ALIVE

You've blown up
your barriers to love,
excavated your heart,
and now it's time to
let that baby
SHINE.

Let your heart's vibrancy pulse, let it beat with aliveness, joy, passion, and love. Your heart was born to be multi-heartgasmic. And your heart knows the way.

TRUST

Doubt Shit Storms

Doubt can be transformed into a helpful friend guiding us to do our best, cheering us on from the sidelines.

Or doubt can be a suffocating monster freezing us in our tracks yelling stuff at us like:

You're going to fail — This isn't going to work — You don't know what you're doing

When the doubt shit storm hits, dive deep.

This is a "mental tsunami"—you know what to do here. Drop into mindfulness. Feel those sensations. Drop the thoughts. Yes, dive your attention down to the sensations in your body.

Anchoring your attention on the sensations keeps you safe from the doubt storm.

When the storm settles, make sure you gather your doubt's wisdom.

Here's how you can mine for your doubt's wisdom:

1. Notice that doubt is present.

2. Close your eyes, place your hand on your heart.

3. Ask, *What are you afraid of?*

4. Consider what's the worst thing that could happen if your fear becomes reality.

5. Consider what would happen if you submit to doubt and don't do anything.

6. If you're committed to whatever the doubt is about, like a goal, make a decision that you will follow through.

7. Then let doubt help guide you in making that goal your reality.

Another way to try this exercise is to make a list of everything you're afraid of. Write down all of the doubts and fears swirling inside your head. This gets our thoughts from our emotional brain out on paper. Then our rational brain can review them.

> Often times, a quick,
> logical look
> is all it takes
> to smash the fear.

Like *I don't know what I'm doing.* Cool, get informed, hire a mentor, educate yourself. Or maybe you can see that you DO know what you're doing.

Or—*I'm going to fail.* Only if you don't try. Or if you choose fear over learning a valuable lesson.

Use mindfulness to duck down out of the storm then gather any wisdom. Maybe you just need guidance, a mentor, or more training. Or perhaps an attitude of *Yes, fear and doubt are here AND I'm going to move forward. My dreams are important enough to me that I'm willing to breathe through these uncomfortable feelings—these little buzzing sensations in my body.*

That's right—living your dreams
requires feeling the occasional,
uncomfortable
body buzz.

Or avoid the buzz and don't live your dreams.

What will you choose??!!

Be Your Own Cheerleader

Do this when you need some extra pep in your step. Or when you're feeling stuck.

Sit with an upright spine and close your eyes. Bring to mind an image of yourself as a child, maybe six or seven years old. See this young you, vibrant, full of life, playing, dancing, and enjoying the world.

If you have a hard time visualizing yourself, bring to mind a photograph you have of yourself from this time period.

This child comes up and hugs you. Then you look into the child's eyes. The child tells you about dreams and fears of not being good enough, of failing, and of having a fear that it won't work out.

What do you say to this beautiful young child?

Find all the words of encouragement that you'd tell this young one. Soothe the child's doubt and kiss the child goodbye for now.

Open your eyes.

You may want to write down these words of encouragement. These are the exact words you can use with yourself when you get caught in a doubt shit storm. Just bring to mind the child who lives within you—the spontaneous ball of joy with big dreams. See this beam of shining young light and let your words of encouragement rip.

> Commit to letting your
> doubt inspire you.

Make this practical by framing a photograph of yourself from this younger age. Place this framed picture on your desk or wherever else feels right. And next time the doubt storm blows through, take a few mindful breaths while gazing at this image of your younger self.

> You can
> reprogram your thinking from
> nasty and unhelpful or paralyzing
> thoughts to beautifully
> encouraging words.

Believe in Yourself

Whatever you believe is true. At least in your world. Because our beliefs inspire our thoughts which inspire our actions which create our experiences.

If you believe you can, you can. Or if you believe you can't, you can't.

BELIEVE YOU CAN!

Because if you believe you're not good enough to get the promotion then the thought might be don't apply for it. The action is doing nothing and the experience is no promotion.

Ultimately, this is your choice.

You can get proactive with your believing. You can reprogram your beliefs.

You can choose to think inspiring thoughts.

Here's why this is important—it's likely that a crap load of what you're believing isn't even what you actually believe. That's right, OPB—*Other People's Beliefs*.

Are you down with OPB?

You've got to SEE what you're believing. Because most likely you've internalized heaps of unhelpful OPBs. And worse, some are harmful.

Affirmations are great for this.

Affirm things you want to believe. Affirm what feels true for you. Affirm things that inspire you to your greatest potential.

If somewhere deep down you took on the OPB that the world is out to get you, flip the script and affirm, *The world is out to enrich me.*

Believe you're unlovable?
Affirm *I am lovable.*

Make a list of affirmations that inspire you. Post them somewhere you can read them at least twice a day. Like in front of your toilet...or on your phone lock screen...or on your computer monitor.

A well-thunk thought becomes a belief, a groove in the brain that then inspires thinking.

Repeat your affirmations as frequently as you can to get that deep groove rocking to the tune of the beliefs you want to believe.

You can also add phrases that inspire you to grow into the person you want to become.
Now go write them down then read them daily.

God's Billboard

To gain confidence and a stronger belief in myself—and
to deepen my faith—I posted this inside my bathroom
medicine cabinet (so I would continually see it):

> Trust your gut,
> even if you don't know why,
> that's where God lives.

Whether you believe in God, the Universe, a Higher
Power or not, you may find that creating a reminder like
this to access a deeper wisdom can have a powerful effect
on your life.

And if God has a billboard to give us life directions, to
answer our prayers, to speak to us—the billboard is
often in our gut.

We can regret NOT listening to our gut.

But I'd take a wild bet that nobody has ever regretted
listening to their gut…

> It's up to us to hone the skill of
> hearing and honoring our intuition—to

> *reading* God's billboard.
> This is an important
> part of learning to
> trust ourselves.

Meditation, of course, helps us hear our intuition better.

For decisions like who to date, where to live, or even what to eat, take a moment to tune in.

Feel into it. Consider what feels right.

Then decide.

Godgasms

Ooo the Godgasm. That chill up your spine. Those goose bumps sprinkling down your arms and legs—"goosies" as my Australian friends say.

The deliciously juicy and fourth dimensional Godgasm!

I believe the chills, the Godgasm, guide us in our deeper purpose in life. Energy floods our system reminding us that we are connected to something greater.

The goosies
let us know that we are
on track, in alignment with
our truth, our soul.

The Godgasm comes when we are connected to Spirit.

Pay attention
to what inspires you,
to what lights your spirit up
with a Godgasmic flood
of energy.

Then decide what it means to you, like do you believe that this is Spirit guiding you?

Is it an indicator that you are "on purpose?" Or is it a signal that what you are thinking or hearing is "your truth?"

Take the time to find out what resonates with you. Befriending your inner guidance and uncovering your calling is intimate.

In the meantime, enjoy the Godgasmic waves of energy.

ELIMINATE

In this section, we'll look at what you may want to remove from your life.

Minimalism

Clear space for the new you, the real you, the you of now. This means letting go of what's no longer serving you. Like those clothes you're never going to wear again, the books you're not going to read or reread, your ancestor's stuff that's just collecting dust.

Yep, toss great-grandma's trinkets.

> If your cup is full of
> the wrong thing, there's no room
> for the right thing.

Room by room, go through your home, and start getting honest.

What are you never going to use again? What will you never wear again? What makes you feel bad when you see it?

Toss it. Give it away, sell it, whatever, just get rid of it.

Let it go.

It may feel uncomfortable—you'll likely feel the anxiety tingles that can come with letting go.

But keeping
something you don't want
and have no use for
to avoid having
a feeling is kinda
odd when
you think about it.

It's just a feeling. Get rid of that stuff.

Notice the stories you create when you cling to stuff you don't use or want. *But this belonged to my dead relative…*or *It was expensive…*or *This will be perfect if I ever get invited to [insert super random event that will likely never happen]…*

Think about it. What do you really want?

Do you want the actual thing or do you want to avoid the feeling of guilt that may come with getting rid of it?

The kicker here is yes, you may feel guilt while letting it go BUT that you are already feeling a constant low-grade guilt for keeping all the stuff you don't want.

The unwanted stuff is taking up psychic space. You can start small and see for yourself. Let a few things go and then see how you feel.

Sell it. Donate it.

If you haven't used it in six months, toss it.

Does that freak you out? Okay, one year. That's a full year including all the seasons.

Or just be totally honest with yourself and if you don't want it, get rid of it.

Period.

Someone else may absolutely love or need the collection of stuff you don't want.

No need to cling to
a scarcity mindset while
getting hits of
bad vibes.

And remember—the world is out to ENRICH you.

Go through your home, your car, your office, your purse, etc.

If you notice anxiety encouraging you to cling to stuff you don't really want or you have no need for, do a second sweep.

Then a third.

A regular
letting go is
good for the
soul.

You may even find that cleaning out your closet is helpful while processing a breakup or another type of loss.

Junk-Free Diet

Gossip is junk. If you want to up your vibe, the gossip has got to stop. It's low vibe.

Gossiping
gives us a slight hit of
superiority, a feeling of
better than.
We don't need that.
We are already
enough.

Finding faults in others probably won't get you to where you want to go in life.

And it's blocking your heart.

Uplifting conversations are likely a better use of your time. Take notice of what you're talking about throughout the day and how you feel afterwards.
If your day is filled with gossip, try dropping it. And it takes two to gossip—even listening to gossip is part of gossiping. This doesn't mean talking about others is always low vibe or cold hearted.

Can you share
an important story
without using
the person's name?
Then drop their name.

Take a look at the magazines or books you read, the television shows you watch, and any other content that you consume.

Garbage in,
garbage out.

If you are feeding your mind on low-vibe stuff, low-vibe stuff will be swirling around inside of you bringing you down. Imagine if you ate pizza for every meal. It'd be insane to also expect to feel good, look good, and to be vibrant and full of energy.

Saturate your mind
in what you want it to be
saturated in—for example,
inspiration, gratitude,
optimism...

Be mindful of what you're choosing to let your mind consume and to when you're feeding on mental junk.

The more conscious we become of the psychic belly ache this junk gives us, the less we'll opt for a mental junk fix.

Friend Detox

We are the company we keep. In a way. Take a good look at who you spend most of your time with.

Could it be that you need to make new friends?

Does chatting with your work buddy leave you feeling yucky? Does your best friend cut you down?

> Having history with someone doesn't mean you're required to also have a future.

Check the present.

Are they supportive? Do you feel cared for? Is the relationship fulfilling? Or is guilt the glue that keeps you together?

This exercise may help guide you in creating mindful friendships.

List everyone you spend time with. Give them one plus if they are a positive person and a second plus if you have a positive relationship with them.

If you want to have positive relationships with positive people, it's up to you to create that. You may decide to keep double negatives in your life—this choice will affect your life force.

Some of us have troubled relationships with family members, in-laws, or bosses. In these cases, we can choose to limit time spent with people that consistently drain us.

Boundaries.

We can try to improve a relationship on our end before walking away.

Bring the person to mind with whom you have a difficult relationship. Pray for them.

Send them mental wishes to have everything you want for yourself—like happiness, health, prosperity, peace of mind, and love.

Everything
is energy—your prayers
are sent like an instantaneous
psychic text.

Whether your friend is conscious of it or not, they are receiving your mental love bomb. You may even get a call from them after you do this!

Changing the relationship in your heart is worth the effort. At the very least it expands your capacity for love. Regardless of what happens with the relationship.

You can choose to have the energy running through you be more important than caring what other people think about you. Contemplate that for a moment.

This is your short and sweet life. May as well CHOOSE who you share it with.

We can all benefit from a reminder from
time to time that we are choosing
way more than we may
consciously
realize.

Divorce Your Story

What is your life like right now?

What's your work like? What's dragging or weighing you down? What's your physical fitness like? What about your social life? What are your hobbies?

Where do you feel stuck?

Consider these questions and then spend 10 minutes writing out your current story.

Keep the emphasis on the parts of your story that aren't what you want or on areas in which you feel stuck.

> What
> would you like to
> eliminate from
> your life?

If you have 10 more minutes, continue with the next exercise, "Have an Affair with your Future Life."

CREATE

In this section, we'll look at what you may want to add to your life, to create.

Have an Affair with Your Future Life

Consider the following questions, then spend 10 minutes writing your "New Story."

Write down the answer to these question in the present tense as if they are already your reality, like *I am in a loving relationship…* Write what you want your life to be like.

> Do not allow fear, doubt, or other limitations to enter your ideal life while journaling.

What do you want your life to be like? What do you ideally want in your friendships? What activities do you share with your friends and what values do you have in common? What do you talk about with your friends?

What about your career—what kind of work do you want to do and what impact do you want your work to have? What types of projects do you work on? Do you work alone or with a team? Do you work in an office, at home, or while traveling around the world? How do you feel when you are at work?

How are you spending your time? How do you want to feel when you wake up? What do you want to do in your free time? What are your hobbies? Where do you live? Do you travel? If so, to where and how often?

What about your love life? Do you want a partner? If so, how do you want to feel in your romantic relationship? How does your partner feel when with you? If you have a partner, answer in terms of what you want to create. What values do you share? What hobbies or activities do you like to do together? Do you have a family?

What is your body like? How is your health? What type of physical activities do you enjoy? Do you go to a gym, yoga, on hikes? What does it feel like to live in your body?

What
else do you
want to
create?

Sexual Ideal

What are you looking for in a romantic partner? Even if you already have one. What do you want—what would your ideal mate be like?

To start, let's get physical. Make a list of what you'd like your future dream babe to be like physically.

Now let's get mental. How is your future dream boat mentally? What's his or her mind like? What character traits does your dream boat have—considerate, patient, punctual?

Next up, emo. List the emotional qualities and aspects of your ideal partner. Is this person even keel, have emotional depth, generous? Is your ideal partner loving and compassionate?

And lastly the spiritual—is faith in a higher power important? How about belief in a particular religion? Will this person meditate with you? List all the spiritual aspects of your ideal babe.

Write this all down before reading on.

Now to the good part…

Go through your lists. And circle everything you're not. Yep, that's right. Plot twist!

If your dream babe is considerate, passionate about life, an athlete and you are not those things—that's your work. Your work is to become those things.

We grow into our ideal.

This is not a *Dear Santa bring me a dream babe* thing.

It's a *Dear Me this is who I want to become* thing.

When you grow into your ideal, you will attract your ideal. We attract what we are.

Go out there and have a blast becoming the ideal qualities you want in your life.

One more thing. Prepare as if you have a houseguest coming. Create space for your babe. Cut inappropriate ties with exes. Take care of yourself.

Behave as if Future Babe is on their way into your life— like you're meeting your soulmate tomorrow.

Hero

Take a couple of moments with your eyes closed.

Bring to mind a hero. This could be an actual superhero, a movie character, or someone you know—like a parent, a mentor, your child, or someone in your community. Look at the qualities of this person that stand out to you. Maybe they were brave in the face of adversity. Perhaps they spoke their truth and stood up for the greater good in their community.

Or maybe they were able to leap tall buildings in a single bound.

Whatever the *super* qualities are, write them down.

You spot it, you got it.

What you admire in someone is likely also in you. Let your recognition of these qualities be your invitation to bring them out in your own life. Start embodying these qualities in your day-to-day life.

> Growing into embodying the
> things that you admire is
> a great spiritual path.

Let these heroes that come to mind wake you up to your own inner superhero. Then strap on your superhero cape and take flight with these qualities.

You-logy

Imagine you are witnessing your own funeral. It's a beautiful ceremony.

Everyone is gathered around celebrating your life. A loved one begins talking, speaking about your magnificent life. What do they say? Or rather, what would you want them to be able to say about you and the life you lived?

What do you want to be known for? What do you want to be remembered by? What legacy do you want to leave? What impact do you want to have?

Consider these questions, then write the eulogy for your own life.

Inspire
yourself to live at
your highest potential.

YOLO

Make a list of everything you want to do in your wild and beautiful life. This is your bucket list. Your YOLO—*You Only Live Once*—list. This is the stuff of your wildest dreams and everything else you desire to do in your lifetime. Open your mind completely, there are no money or time or other limitations invited into this process.

Maybe this will get your juices flowing:

> Jump out of an airplane, safari in Africa, volunteer at an overseas orphanage, climb a volcano, swim with dolphins, grow vegetables, travel to the other side of the world, do a color run or half marathon, road trip across America, write a book, fly in a hot air balloon, share your life's message on the TEDx stage, make a snowman, learn a foreign language, reconnect with a family member, learn how to knit, visit the Taj Mahal, go camping, fall in love, go to Disneyland, bungee jump, ride a horse, graduate, launch a business…

Keep adding to this list over the next week and beyond. And maybe one day you'll knock out your bucket list.

Because YOLO.

Feeling Foreplay

How do you want to feel? Energized, confident, happy, loved, vibrant…?

Often, when we have a goal like get married or earn lots of money, what we actually want is a feeling. Like a desire to feel loved and cared for or to feel stable and secure.

Start by considering some of your goals. Then look underneath them.

What feelings do you imagine that achieving that goal will bring? Write those feelings down.

Now that you've cut out the middle man, see if you can hang out in those feelings a bit more. Meaning daily.

Visualize yourself feeling those feelings.

> ## It's a total win-win when you can cultivate those feelings WHILE you're achieving those goals.

Deliberately hanging out in the feelings we want to feel will attract more of those feelings into our life.

Vision Board

Grab some magazines and flip through them. Find images that represent the life you want to live. Places, relationships, words…

> Get the look and feel down—the
> vision, the vibe—for the
> life you want
> to live.

Hang your vision board somewhere that you'll see it regularly. Then your subconscious mind can get to work, helping to make this vision your reality.

It's like if you bought a red truck—suddenly you see red trucks everywhere. It's not that everyone else instantly got a red truck too, it's that your mind started to notice them.

Make the collage and then your subconscious mind will do its thing to help turn your vision into your reality.

This is powerful; don't skip this one.

Creative Visualization

Manifesting babe.

Get into a comfortable, seated position and close your eyes. Take several mindful breaths. Focus on the air going into and out of your nostrils.

Then start to visualize what you want. Let's say you want to be a mother. Visualize yourself pregnant, nursing, and raising a child. Imagine all the details associated with this.

Use all of your senses.

Hang out in the emotion of what you want. How do you feel as a mother? Feel those feelings. When we feel the feelings of what we want, we attract it into our lives. It's energy. I'm not saying that visualizing yourself pregnant will get you pregnant but it may have you switch up how you date or who you are attracting into your love life.

Repeat this.

Bathe your body in the energy of what you want to attract.

The Good Feels

Swim in gratitude. Again, we attract what we feel, so practice bringing your mind to feeling grateful for what you have.

> Then you'll feel good
> AND attract more of
> what feels good.

Feeling upset or wronged or lacking something comes naturally. Literally. It's our caveman or cavewoman brain "keeping us safe." This part of our brain is always on the lookout for "danger" and is great at spotting "what's wrong."

This keeps us alive when there's actually danger. Like when that saber tooth tiger cruises by.

This keeps us miserable when our mind is a fault-finding factory.

> Flip the script
> and spot what's right!

Try this. Each morning, make, a list of 5-10 things you're grateful for. Write next to each thing WHY you are grateful for it.

After you've got your list and your whys, reread your list. And feeeeeeeeeel it.

Pause after each one and drop into how grateful you feel for what you wrote.

Boom. You've just rocked your world.

Pillow Talk

This is a continuation on gratitude.

Each night when your head hits your pillow, do a mental gratitude list. Count on your fingers 10 things you're grateful for that happened in your day.

Yea, literally use your fingers.

Then slip off into a grateful sleep, basking in good vibes. Which of course may bring you more good vibes.

And super-sweet dreams.

THE REVOLUTION

You've come so far on your heartgasmic journey—the journey to living a life filled with joy, passion, love and aliveness! The more you clear away what's been blocking your heart and tune into what your heart desires, the more explosive with LIFE you'll become.

The REVOLUTION this book
has been guiding you towards
is a revolution inside
your heart.

As you go throughout your day, keep some of your attention tuned into your heart. What makes your heart beat faster? What resonates with your heart? What does your heart want more of? What makes your heart explode with rapture?

Let the wisdom of your heart
be your north star, guiding your
actions and steering your life.

One heartgasm at a time.

P.S. THE DOUBLE CHECK

There's one more thing I want to leave you with.

This is your go-to practice for personal power.

I call this "THE DOUBLE CHECK," and it's the most transformative thing I could teach you at this point in my journey.

It's a combination of what we've already covered, it's super simple, and it's immediately worked 100% of the time for me and my clients to take us from an emotionally intense place including overwhelmed to a place of power, choice, and freedom.

Yes, the former statistician is making a bold claim.

And it's 100% true.

1. Check your thoughts.

They're likely NOT true. When you notice a thought that is blocking your progress, your dream, your happiness, check it. Is it true? Is it helpful? Simply having the space to notice the thought helps create a buffer from actually believing it.

2. Check your feels.

After you check your thoughts, drop your attention into your body and notice the sensations. Where are the sensations? How big are they?

Whether we call it frustration, anger, anxiety, doubt, etc., what my clients usually say is that they notice sensations either in their chest, belly, or throat that are the size of a basketball, a softball, or an apple. (For some reason, it's always sports equipment or fruit!)

Once you name the size of the sensations, open your eyes and take a breath.

Then close your eyes, clear your mind, and check again.

What size are the sensations now?

My clients usually report a "basketball" becoming a "golf ball" or an "apple" becoming a "grape."

The grape or "it's gone completely" is unbelievably common across the people I've taken through this on the double check.

This means the sensations we call "angry" or "overwhelmed" lessened in INTENSITY and in SIZE or dissolved completely in the short time it took to take a breath and check again.

This is next f*cking level empowering.

To experience how our awareness of the sensations—just noticing what IS without seeking to change it— changes the sensations in a way that we prefer.

Our consciousness changes matter.

In real time.
Real quick.
Every time.

THIS IS YOUR MOFO SUPER POWER.

The double check.

Double check your thoughts.

Then double check your feels.

Every time
I've guided a client
through this, they seem to be
bedazzled by their power
to shift their internal world just
by noticing and allowing it.

"The basketball is a golf ball!" Or "The apple is gone!"

Its simplicity, reliability, and effectiveness bedazzles me too—I mean, I'm the kinda woman who spent 17 years slowly killing myself with booze out of, in a way, an unwillingness and inability to feel my feels.

This is how
I broke free from
my secondary addictions
in sobriety.

By learning how to love myself, by feeling my feels—like literally noticing the sensations and allowing them to be as they are.

I transformed my relationship with physical pain the same way.

> When we meet our sensations with our awareness, we transform our entire world.

The next time you feel the urge to engage in a secondary addiction, or find yourself overwhelmed with emotion...

If you're into prayer, pray.

Then reach for the double check.

> This mind-blowing practice moves us from a place of victimhood and resistance to the seat of choice to consider, *What do I actually want?*

This is true freedom.

AFTERWORD

I wrote this book in Ubud, Bali back in February 2017. A couple months later, I felt called to leave Bali and to go to America to speak about long-term effects of unhealed childhood sexual abuse. I was terrified to answer this call, yet it was so loud and clear and important that I dropped everything to answer it.

The calling took front stage of my life and led to the TEDx stage where I connected the dots between early sexual trauma and subsequent poor mental health and addiction (if you're interested, you can watch the talk here: kirjohnson.com/tedtalk).

In the meantime, this sassy book took a looong nap on my laptop.

Flash forward to two years after writing this book, and after a lot of editing, *The Heartgasm Revolution* was ready to come alive and be published.

> I was ready to come alive too,
> quite frankly.

I love my work, but at the end of the day, most of it was really just me, sitting home alone on my laptop or on coaching calls, day after day. I feared that learning how to launch this book would have me even more isolated on my laptop. Which is the opposite of what I wanted this book (and my life!) to be infused with.

This book was intended to be FUN. I wanted to have fun.

So I decided to switch things and get out of the house. I hired a camera crew to follow me around to create a YouTube show—which felt super awkward at first.

We filmed episode one in Uluwatu, Bali. I was floating in the ocean on a paddle board and a dad with two young kids looked over at me, then up at the drone above my head, then back at me and said, "Who are you?!"

Feeling awkward AF, I replied,

"No one. I'm nobody. Just a girl with a dream..."

A dream to have FUN while learning how to publish a book and become a speaker.

If you're like me, if you have a message to share with the world, a change you want to make, and you want to speak and or write books, then my show was created with you in mind.

Come along with me as I get waaaaaaay outside my comfy zone befriending speakers I admire, asking them their advice on how to get into speaking while also having fun on the journey of publishing a book. I got to hang out in some amazing places and with some amazing people—showing me that it's wild what can happen when you just decide to SHOW UP for your dreams and reach out.

But to be clear, fear and doubt showed up too!

Creating the YouTube show made obvious to me again—that fear and doubt don't go away, and that if they've been at bay for a while, maybe just maybe it's a clue that we've been playing small.

The speakers I interview in the show all said the same thing—that the fear and doubt haven't left them, but that they've become better at showing up for their dreams despite it being there.

You can watch my YouTube show, "Come Alive" here: kirjohnson.com/heartgasm

ACKNOWLEDGEMENTS

I close my eyes and think of all of the support, encouragement, and inspiration I've received over the years since my first spiritual awakening, getting sober in 2009. Realizing the magnitude of people, whether I've ever met them personally or not, that have influenced my soul's evolution melts my heart into a gentle explosion of gratitude and love, a sweet and subtle heartgasm.

Big thank you to my first sponsor Lisa K. for pointing me to spirit each time I showed up in victim mode. Another big thank you to Gabby Bernstein who, through being herself at her book launch in 2011, showed me that writing and speaking about spirituality could be a career. It was at that little Corte Madera book store, while watching her speak, that I heard, "THIS is what you do!" Which was confusing AF to hear because at the time I was a statistician and terrified of public speaking.

Thank you, Marisa Ravel and Melinda Ronald, for bringing so much joy to my life—you have been the bright spot of my life for years and inspired the chapters on God's Billboard and the Godgasm.

Extra special thanks Marisa, for naming the subtitle of this book. And I just about died of a massive heartgasm when you added the holographic magical background to the cover—it's beyond my wildest dreams. Thank you for making the cover sparkle and pop. You inspire me.

Thank you to the people who helped me behind the scenes to bring this book to life: my editor Rebecca Dettorre who patiently waited on my reply while I was on my 13,000 mile USA road trip and frequently off the grid; my test readers who gave me invaluable feedback including my dad Nels Johnson for inspiring me make the book gender neutral, Kylee Marie, Stephanie Robinson, Lauren Reid, Petra Fant, and Jacqueline Fifield; my cover photographer Brian Crawford for an amazing photo shoot including getting in the pool to take the cover shot, and cover designer Giovanni Rossi for the initial cover design and customizing the title font.

Thank you to Gretchen, my younger sister. I am so inspired by watching you chase and live your dreams as a fashion designer. I feel honored to be wearing one of your gorgeous UNSUPERVISED Los Angeles outfits in the cover shot on this book. I'm your biggest fan.

Special thanks again to my dad Nels Johnson for always encouraging me to write, for helping me edit the first draft of this book, and for showing me what unconditional love looks like. Your support means the world to me and I feel so lucky to be loved by you.

There has been much inspiration for the content of this book and many people to thank.

During my own deep heart healing journey, I read hundreds of books and attended dozens if not hundreds of workshops and retreats across the world. After emerging from my healing, I thought long and hard about what had helped me heal the most, what practices and tools were the most transformative, whether they'd come from other teachers or I'd intuitively started doing them myself. This book is the result of those best practices.

The mentors, teachers, and friends that inspired some of the exercises are: Cary Fortin for minimalism, Karen Kimsey House for bonding with trees, Rick Cowley for the hero and You-logy, and Matak Chia for smiling at our organs.

Thank you to my virtual mentors, whom I've never met but whose work I contemplated for years: Wayne Dyer, John Bradshaw, Eckhart Tolle, Jack Kornfield, Marianne Williamson, Bill Wilson, Osho, Buddha for Metta Loving Kindness and Tonglen meditations, and Rumi for poetry about the heart.

Thank you to Jessie, my boyfriend at the time I wrote this in February 2017, a big-hearted man who believed in me and always encouraged me to write. And Bali, Island of the Gods, a piece of land that somehow inspires me to feel more of my heart, the corner of Earth where my soul feels most at home. Bali is my happy place. Thank you, Bali, for allowing me to live, love, and transform on your land. I am forever grateful for all that you've given me. *Suksma.*

And thank you to Blackstreet and Dr. Dre for their song "No Diggity." One day, a year and a half before I wrote this book, I was sitting in Kafe, a restaurant in Ubud, Bali, contemplating what had happened in my heart. I thought of the rapture and deep grief I felt when I'd first visited Bali while looking at the palm trees. Then the song "No Diggity" came on and when I heard the word "eargasm" sung, I had a silly A-ha moment. Heartgasm! Heartgasm was the name of what had been happening in my heart. And with that, a seed was planted for this sassy book.

Books that Inspired the Healing of My Heart and Some of the Practices in this Book

Radical Acceptance: Embracing Your Life with the Heart of a Buddha, Tara Brach

Healing the Shame that Binds You, John Bradshaw

The Success Principles: How to Get from Where You Are to Where You Want to Be, Jack Canfield

There's a Spiritual Solution to Every Problem, Wayne W. Dyer

New Minimalism: Decluttering and Design for Sustainable, Intentional Living, Cary Telander Fortin and Kyle Louise Quilici

Creative Visualization: Use the Power of Your Imagination to Create What You Want in Your Life, Shakti Gawain

Emotional Intelligence: Why It Can Matter More Than IQ, Daniel Goleman, Ph.D.

You Can Heal Your Life, Louise L. Hay

Loving What Is: Four questions that can change your life, Byron Katie

A Path with Heart: A Guide Through the Perils and Promises of Spiritual Life, Jack Kornfield

The Desire Map: A Guide to Creating Goals with Soul, Danielle LaPorte

Anatomy of the Spirit: The Seven Stages of Power and Healing, Caroline Myss, Ph.D.

The Untethered Soul: The Journey Beyond Yourself, Michael A. Singer

The Power of Now: A Guide to Spiritual Enlightenment, Eckhart Tolle

A Return to Love: Reflections on the Principles of A COURSE IN MIRACLES, Marianne Williamson

Alcoholics Anonymous, Bill Wilson

The Seat of the Soul, Gary Zukav

COMING SOON

Elephant

A memoir by Kirsten Johnson

Stay updated on upcoming books and other exciting things by joining Kirsten's mailing list here: kirjohnson.com

ABOUT THE AUTHOR

Kirsten Johnson is a life coach and motivational speaker. She holds a bachelor's degree in psychology from San Francisco State University and a master's in statistics from the University of California at Los Angeles. She worked for high-tech startups and headed the fraud division at eBay for a time.

Kirsten launched her coaching business in 2012 and is a professional certified coach through the International Coach Federation. She is committed to living a life beyond her wildest dreams and helps others across the world do the same through her online programs and courses, a YouTube channel, and private coaching.

Kirsten, 42, is a native of Marin County, California. She has been traveling the world as a digital nomad since 2014 and currently lives in Bali, Indonesia.

You can find, follow, friend and tag Kirsten here:

Facebook.com/KirstenJohnsonXo
Instagram.com/KirstenJohnsonXo
Youtube.com/KirstenJohnsonXo

#heartgasm

Share the self love.

If you feel inspired to share this book—please do. Lend it to a friend or send them a copy.

Heartgasms for everyone!

Made in the USA
San Bernardino, CA
09 September 2019